Stories That Heal

By the same author

Stories for the Third Ear

Selections from Stories for the Third Ear
(audiotape)

A NORTON PROFESSIONAL BOOK

Stories That Heal

REPARENTING ADULT CHILDREN OF
DYSFUNCTIONAL FAMILIES USING
HYPNOTIC STORIES IN PSYCHOTHERAPY

LEE WALLAS

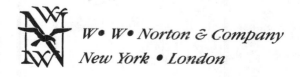

W• W• Norton & Company
New York • London

Library of Congress Cataloging-in-Publication Data

Wallas, Lee.
    Stories that heal : reparenting adult children of dysfunctional
families using hypnotic stories in psychotherapy / Lee Wallas.
       p.   cm.
    "A Norton professional book."
    ISBN 0-393-70106-9
    1. Adult children of dysfunctional families—Rehabilitation.
2. Storytelling—Therapeutic use.   3. Hypnotism—Therapeutic use.
I. Title.
RC455.4.F3W34   1991   616.89'14—dc20   90-46354
                                                  CIP

W. W. Norton & Company, Inc., 500 Fifth Avenue, New York, N.Y. 10110

W. W. Norton & Company Ltd., 10 Coptic Street, London WC1A 1PU

  2 3 4 5 6 7 8 9 0

This book is dedicated to
my mother and father,
who did the best they could.

Contents

CONTENTS

Epilogue

Prologue: Elsewhere

There is all around you a familiar, unfamiliar landscape. It seems almost three-dimensional. It's all one color. There are no shadows. There seem to be no objects. It just seems to be a wonderful floating space. In that space, your feelings are very calm, dreamlike, comfortable, weightless. At the edge of this area there is an aperture. It appears to be guarded by two figures that you can make out dimly, and somehow you recognize that they are your conscious and your unconscious. Your conscious wears a garment of many changing colors. And your unconscious sometimes seems to be one figure, and another time another figure, seems to be changing, gradually becoming one, and then the other, and then back again, and then, perhaps, a third and a fourth, and back again, and you understand that the unconscious has many interchangeable coordinated parts, and you watch this with fascination. You approach the aperture and you see that it seems to be covered by an opaque film. Or at least it seems opaque, until you get close, and you see that it is, in fact, translucent but not transparent. And you see that you cannot enter the elsewhere space. You talk to your conscious mind, and you ask if you may enter there, and your conscious mind turns away, unhearing. You ask your unconscious mind, "May I enter there?" And your unconscious mind says, "No, not yet." Then you say, "May I see what lies behind the opening?" and, without a reply, the translucent film fades away. You look into a space that is the marvelous blue-purple of elsewhere. Then it changes and becomes other colors, beautiful colors that come from you. You watch with wonder, as you look into that space, and see the beautiful, slowly evolving colors. And there is a sound, a rhythmic sound, like a muffled drum that goes BOOM, boom, BOOM, boom, BOOM, boom. You take great comfort in the sound, great comfort. You find yourself drawn to that beautiful space. Both your conscious and your unconscious stand aside as, head first, you drift into elsewhere.

Stories That Heal

Introduction

Margaret Mead wrote her autobiography, *Blackberry Winter*, as an example of how children could be parented. In it she quotes a childhood friend who said to her, "In my house I was a child; in your family's house I was a person." She writes, "In this book I have tried to describe the kinds of experiences that have made me what I am, myself, and to sort out the kinds of experiences that might become part of a way of bringing up children . . . [so as] to throw what light it may on how children can be brought up so that parents and children, together, can weather the roughest seas."[1]

Later, in *Culture and Commitment*, she continues, " . . . we can construct an environment in which a child . . . can be safe and can grow and discover itself and the world. . . . they must be held or propped up or cradled. . . . As their eyes respond to color, there must be many colors. . . . There must be many kinds of objects for them to classify, many rhythms and melodies to start them dancing. . . . And . . . they must . . . be given crayons and paints and clay so they can give form to the world of their own imaginations.

"Even so simple an enumeration of ways of meeting a child's needs makes us conscious of how much children have been bound to the ways of their forebears through love and dependence and trust. . . . The child is wholly dependent, and it is on this dependency that human culture has been built as, generation after generation . . . adults have imposed on children, through their care for them, their vision of what life should be."[2]

Surely there have been many adults who parent their children in this way, but of course those children do not come to me for treatment. The "grown-up children" who come to see me have had entirely different parenting. They talk, almost without exception, about an unhappy childhood (or a totally blacked-out childhood), about a miserable adolescence, and about confused, frustrated adult lives. Of course, "adult children" often tell me about alcoholism and/or co-dependency, but I also hear about workaholics, gamblers, substance abusers, other addicts with eating disorders, and about stress-related illnesses, migraines, heart problems, ulcers, cancer, asthma, allergies, or about physical abuse, and psychological abuse, about incest, about neuroses, and about psychoses. What I hear is the comprehensive story of dysfunctional families. And although the focus of research and treatment has been largely directed towards adult children of alcoholics, my own clinical experience indicates that alcoholism is only one of the dysfunctions which can and do affect families and their "adult children."

Most of the adult children I have treated seem to suffer similar effects of trauma. They experience feelings of confusion, guilt, shame, anger, and fear in varying degrees. Often they complain about having been deprived of a childhood. They were too busy taking on adult functions, substituting for their inadequate parents, trying to keep their families intact; they were often too busy just trying to survive. They felt unloved and now they feel unlovable. "If my mother (or father, or both) didn't love me, then there must be something very wrong, very bad about me." They become "caretakers" to get love for what they can do for others, since they believe they are not lovable for themselves.

Claudia Black has described three basic rules that prevail in such families: Don't talk, don't trust, don't feel.[3] Children of dysfunctional families often grow up unable to identify their feelings and so are unable to deal with them. As a result they take refuge in deep denial. Early on they learn that it is not safe to trust people. And so, unable to trust, to share, or to accept empathy, they are shut off from intimacy and spontaneity. In order to avoid disappointment and rejection, they learn not to ask for anything. Some learn to make themselves "invisible," and in order not to "rock the boat" they agree with anyone and everyone. They become quiet and unobtrusive. They feel incapable of making decisions. They believe they have no power to make changes in themselves or their lives.

Others learn to be "controllers." They become rigid, obsessive, fearful of any change. They try to control everyone and everything in their lives in order to maintain the status quo, to avoid change. They

[4]

think in terms of black/white, either/or, with no options between the extremes. Sometimes they doubt their own sanity since what happened in their families often made no sense. So they conclude that they are the ones who are incapable of making sense in their own lives. I have come to the conclusion that all traumatized adult children share the same syndrome, and that "adult children of dysfunctional families" most accurately describes them.

I myself am an adult child of a dysfunctional family. When I was in graduate school I wrote a paper entitled, "The Effects of Being the Child of Motherless Parents." We were studying developmental stages in a course taught by a psychiatrist trained in psychoanalysis. Recently, upon rereading my paper, I was struck by how many of the classical theories of the developmental stages, their tasks, and the consequences of unsuccessfully negotiating passage from one stage to the next are now being applied to adult children of dysfunctional families. That is why I think it would be pertinent to share with you my paper, written years ago, about my own experience as the child of a dysfunctional family.[4]

THE EFFECTS OF BEING THE CHILD
OF MOTHERLESS PARENTS

Neither of my parents had incorporated a superego sufficient for parenting a child. Both my maternal and paternal grandmothers died in giving birth to my parents. Each child had a busy, harassed father who married immediately after the death of his first wife. My mother had a 12-year-old sister and two older brothers; my father had a seven-year-old sister and an older brother. There were many babies born to the two stepmothers, and I have been told that their parents were too harried to pay much attention to either my mother or my father. My paternal aunt told me that my father was always incorrigible—truant, fighting, and repeatedly running away from home. When he was 16 he ran away to the United States and never again returned to his family in Austria. His sister had preceded him here. My maternal aunt and uncles brought my mother to the United States when she was 15. She never returned home to Russia either. Both my parents were illiterate in English. They went to work in a factory, and met when she was 17 and he was 24. When she got pregnant, her sister forced them to marry. I was born two months before my mother's 18th birthday. My mother describes her labor as lasting through three

[5]

days of agony. When she began to nurse me she developed breast abscesses. My parents fought wildly with each other from the beginning.

My earliest memories are of yelling and cursing and blows. My mother tells me I was a "devil" and screamed constantly. What must have happened was that I was not sufficiently shielded from overstimulation resulting from the turmoil in the household and my mother's emotional distress. I had basic survival fears, with good reason. Certainly, the situation, my mother's ignorance, compounded by her pain and resentment around nursing with abscessed breasts, prevented me from completing the tasks of the autistic and symbiotic phases. I did accomplish a good physiological extrauterine homeostasis, but the developmental failure was that I experienced basic fear because of the threat against my survival, about which more later. Genetically I must have been very healthy because I did not develop infantile psychosis.

I believe that I sustained a subconscious psychic trauma in the autistic phase because of my mother's poor holding, in addition to her ineffectual protection against overstimulation. Perhaps I shall never entirely overcome my underlying sense of vague, unnamed danger, as well as my recurrent feelings of depression ever-ready to surface in adversity.

The symbiotic phase was even more traumatic. I think that I began to separate earlier than is usual because of my mother's unpredictability. I had to be my own mother. I have no conscious memory of her until after I was five years old. The reason I conclude that there was unsatisfactory symbiosis stems from my fears about the reaction of strangers to me, which even now reappear occasionally, although in no way in the exaggerated degree of my adolescence. During adolescence I had strong feelings of panic when people would leave me or if I thought I was being excluded. Even now I sometimes feel afraid under these circumstances.

I have no memory of the rapprochement phase. I had probably resigned myself to having "lost the love" of my mother. I reconstruct this because of later feelings that "there is something wrong with me and I am unlovable." That I introjected the "bad mother" image was confirmed by my temper tantrums. The task of the rapprochement phase, which is to retain or restore self-esteem in the context of the relative constancy of a loving parent as well as to maintain a unified self-image based on good ego identification, remained unresolved. There is a photograph of me when I was 18 months old. I am sitting rigidly upright, with an expression of fixed watchfulness, unsmiling and frozen.

I hatched and began practicing early. I think I was eager to be independent of mother. I crawled and walked before I was one year old, and I was talking in sentences very early. I am told that I was very bright and could name all the colors before I was two. When I was an adult I asked my mother about my toilet training. She said I had a little potty (we had no inside plumbing, which was probably a lucky break for me) and she thought I learned by myself because she didn't remember anything about it.

I had a very low frustration tolerance, a very bad temper, and would stage frequent tantrums during which I would throw myself to the floor and kick and scream at the top of my lungs. For this my father would beat me black and blue. The beatings did not stop me, and I was considered "stubborn as a mule." I have completely repressed this period in my life. These stories were told to me later on by my mother and my aunt. I still have a low frustration point, although I am much more under control. I still sometimes feel unreasonably enraged, but now I can find acceptable ways to let off steam.

My memories of my father when I was in the oedipal phase are quite vivid. Once I saw his penis and remember feeling full of shame, frustration and fear. Although my mother walked about naked, he never did. He often said, "Shame on you." I thought there was something secret and dangerous he was hiding. I was afraid of him, but at the same time I wanted his love. He would alternately hold me too close and kiss me too wetly, or else push me away and hit me. I believed that he loved me. It wasn't until I was a grown woman that I understood that he had no love to give. I was irrationally sure he would take care of me if I ever needed anything. He represented security to me, yet I felt ashamed and afraid around him. I also felt guilty, as though I, too, had something to hide, but didn't know what it was.

My mother's body was fat and I hated her big breasts and buttocks. My father's body was neat and compact like mine. I think I knew very clearly that I was a girl, but I wanted to be like him as much as possible. My father didn't like my mother, so I wouldn't be like her. I would be like him.

Fortunately, I had two surrogate parents. One was Mammy Green, a big, warm, rough Black woman who sometimes took care of me. I don't remember much except being bathed and scolded. The memory is comfortable. The other was my paternal aunt, who had a strong superego (she was of Freud's generation) and interested herself in my rearing. I would spend many weekends with her. She was widowed, so there was no man in her house. This Victorian lady taught me prissy manners and propriety. In spite of my parents' disdain for her, I sensed her love and concern for me, and I believe that I gained some stability and sex-role identification from her role modeling.

My first days at school were anxious. When a little girl told my kindergarten teacher that I made her late for school, I felt terrified and cried hysterically. When in the first grade my front tooth fell out, I sat on it all day and wouldn't get up. I thought I would be punished. When I heard that the second grade teacher hit children with a ruler, I had to be dragged to her room. My defense against anxiety was to become excessively compliant. My mother called me a "house devil and a street angel." I became a perfect goody-two-shoes at school.

When I was five I discovered the magic world of books. From that time on I was deaf and blind to my parents. I buried myself in books. There I found my role models. I entered the second stage of latency with the joy and exuberance reminiscent of the late "practicing" phase. I was in love with school and books and other little girls. I fell in love with my third grade teacher, and I believe she loved me back. I felt successful. She gave me a "new" geography book because I was a good student. She showed off my poems to the other teachers. I asked her to come home with me and teach my mother how to read and write. And she said, "Yes!" She did come two or three times, but my mother was too embarrassed and stopped the lessons. I told my mother that if she didn't learn to read we wouldn't have anything to talk to each other about when I grew up. And that is what happened. I was eight years old, parenting my mother, and still trying to establish symbiosis with her.

I had two girlfriends. The three of us were inseparable. We were the smartest kids in the class. We jumped rope and wrote skits for the other kids. We had secrets and whispered about how gross the boys were, and some of the tomboys too. I was afraid of the tough kids who got into fights and trouble. I spent my time after school either at the library or at my friend Ruth's house. She had three sisters, a big, calm mother, and a quiet father. I came often and stayed late; I remember looking at the moon as I walked home. My mother didn't care, and my father rarely came home for supper anymore.

These were very happy years for me. My sense of self-esteem, so weak and unstable, was strengthened and reinforced by my successes and achievements at school. My parents were no longer the barometer of my self-esteem. My superego was modified by incorporating other, more supportive parent figures. My attitudes and values were being formed by kind and predictable teachers and by marvelous books. I had a secure alliance with my two inseparable loyal friends, so that my needs for closeness and intimacy and trust were being met for the first time.

When I was almost 11 I began a flirtation with the 12-year-old boy next door. We wrote each other notes in a code we invented. De-coded, his notes usually read, "Do you love me?" and mine read, "Lvf" which decoded to "Yes." This went on mostly by written word for several months. We had few actual face-to-face encounters. One evening when both my parents were out, Johnny came over. I was in my pajamas and robe. Johnny kissed me. It was a child's kiss. My father came home, was very angry to find Johnny there, and sent him home. I confessed that we had kissed, and my father flew into a rage. He went over to Johnny's house to confront his parents and to forbid Johnny to speak to me ever again. That night I heard my parents yelling and screaming about it. I felt covered with shame and guilt.

I completed the eighth grade when I was 12. In those days bright students skipped grades and graduated early. I was sent away to a girls' boarding school. My teacher helped me choose the school. It was a first-rate academically accredited school. But from the point of view of my emotional needs it could not have been worse. It had a female headmistress, a spinster with a degree from Oxford Universi-ty, an early feminist. There was one man on campus: the caretaker (who bore absolutely no resemblance to Lady Chatterley's lover). Everyone else was female, and the majority of the staff must have been virgins. Although there was a solid academic curriculum, sex education was conspicuous by its absence. There were two levels of existence: the social level in which there was no sex acknowledged, and the thick, excited, sexual turmoil of 300 young women that boiled under the surface and produced its own secret subculture. School rules were strict. Boys could visit on Saturday afternoon from 2 to 5 o'clock. We could meet with them in a parlor chaperoned by a teacher. If we were caught smoking or drinking we were immediately expelled, period. The school was situated in the country, 15 miles from the nearest town. We were not permitted to have a car. A dance was held once a year to which were invited the young men from a military school 15 miles away. I started school in January. The first dance was scheduled for St. Valentine's Day. The afternoon of the dance I started my first menstrual period. My roommate, aged 16, *showed me what to do. I felt scared and ashamed. She also showed me how to put on lipstick. No cadet wrote his name on my dance card, and after an agonized hour, I escaped to the restroom, where I stayed until the dance was over.*

At 12, I was the youngest student in the school. Everyone else was at least 14 or older. Nobody wanted to be friends with the "baby." My 16-year-old roommate avoided me whenever possible. I would make up stories about my "boyfriend" at home. All the other girls talked about their hot love affairs with boys at home. I felt confused, dislocated, and not-belonging. I was filled with nameless longing and unhappiness. I began to develop big breasts like my mother and I hated my body (no longer neat and simple like my father's): still unresolved oedipal conflicts. Everything about me seemed wrong. I felt like an outcast, excluded.

It was at this time that I learned that my parents were divorced. My mother telephoned me to tell me her new address. My father sent a dictated note about his new apartment. There was no room for me at either place. I don't remember feeling distress or anxiety about their divorce at that time. So many of the other girls at school had "broken" homes that perhaps I regarded my parents' divorce as more or less normal.

My adolescence was spent between boarding school and summer camp in Maine. I never saw my parents except for a week or so at holidays. When I was 15 my father remarried. His wife was 22 and pregnant. I felt shock and despair. My safety in the world seemed irreparably gone. Separation anxiety took over. I experienced his remarriage as a final loss; there would be, forever, something missing in me. I increased my activities and achievements. I became one of the best swimmers and hockey players. I ranked first in my classes. I consistently won the poetry prizes. I was one of the best artists. I maintained an attitude of aloof superiority. It was of paramount importance to appear not to need anyone, to be self-sufficient. I lived in a world of books, which I read at night by flashlight under the covers. At summer camp I reverted to latency, carefree activity, and OK-ness. There I had close friends with whom to giggle and share secrets.

By the time I was 17, I had completed high school and two years of college at the boarding school. I had lived the entire period between 12 and 17 without once getting to know a young man. I sublimated my adolescent task of making a decisive turn toward heterosexuality. I gyrated between symbiotic strivings, separation-individuation prob-

lems, oedipal conflicts, and latency. Everything was filtered through my unresolved early developmental phases.

I experienced all the typical adolescent phases but in an exaggerated way. At 15 I became exaltedly religious, going to the woods alone to pray on my knees in the damp leaves, experiencing chills of transcendence in chapel, forcing my "lady-bountiful do-goodism" on unwilling misfits among my classmates. At 16 I transformed myself into a coldly intellectual atheist. I became the advocate of the oppressed, of civil rights, and the foe of the "degenerate rich." I was a passionate and grandiose debater. For most of that year I carried a copy of Proust in French under my arm; I also wrote away for an unexpurgated edition of Boccaccio, which was confiscated at the school post office. The headmistress called me an iconoclast. I had to look it up in the dictionary.

When I was 18 I went to Paris to study painting with Andre Lhote, a renowned teacher at that time. My mother gave me the money when she heard that my father had forbidden me to go. I stayed in Paris for four years. It was an exciting time in many ways, but basically I felt anonymous (identity and separation-individuation issues) and as though I did not belong anywhere (symbiosis issue). I made many friends from many different countries and incorporated values from them. I had a single sexual encounter with a man, which scared me. The next day I asked a friend, "Is that all?" My four years in France were a continuation of my adolescence, without resolution. I did learn to speak French fairly well, and I learned how to paint.

When I returned to the United States I met my husband. He fell in love with me and I married him. I liked him but I was not "in love" with him, although I pretended to be. I wanted to get out of my father's household where I was living miserably with him and his young wife whom I hated (shades of Oedipus again). My husband was a kind man, and gentle with me, but I felt cold and shut off sexually. I had a great deal to resolve still, before I would be ready for mature love. Once again, my own parents' lack of role models for love relationships translated into my own deficits. We planned for both our children. When my son was born I felt overjoyed, but I proved to be an anxious mother, following to the letter the ridiculous rules that were fashionable in the 1930s. My baby would cry and I would cry with him, but he did not get nursed until the clock hand hit the four-hour limit. I tried to toilet train him at six months! Fortunately, he was a robust and good-natured baby.

I was with my son constantly until he was three, and we had a good time together. Perhaps I had observed my own mother nursing my infant brother, although I have no conscious memory of that period. I know that she loved him very much because her behavior toward him later on was very loving. Possibly she was a role model for me with my own son. At any rate, when my daughter was born three years later, although we were overjoyed when she arrived, my reactions were very different. I developed breast abscesses when nursing her, just as my mother had done! I did not want to be constantly with her the way I had been with my son. I felt preoccupied and irritable, even though she was a darling infant and I loved her. I think I must have been reenacting my own infancy. I felt guilty and miserable.

That is when I began therapy with a psychoanalyst. I changed enough, in time, to comfortably form mature relationships. My husband and I were married 33 years before he died. We worked out a good partnership with a lot of mutual caring. I am reasonably free of anxiety, and I have matured sexually. I occasionally feel many of the old insecurities, but with much less intensity and for very short duration in time. My children are grown and have families of their own. I relived each of my developmental stages with them as they progressed through each of theirs. My children are fine people. My husband and I must have done quite a few things that were all right. I lead a full life with exciting goals, lots of fun, and many satisfactions. I know how to accept my feelings and my disappointments. I hope to live a very long time because there is a lot I want to do. I like being here, and I like myself most of the time.

In conclusion, I think I might have perpetuated the syndromes my parents suffered because they lacked parenting, except for my fortunate access to substitute parenting from my aunt and Mammy Green, as well as the excellent role modeling available to me during latency. My infatuation with books opened worlds to me that were closed to my parents. That I had the sense to go for help at last was largely due to education. I feel very fortunate.

REPARENTING

Partly because of my own personal experience, and largely because of my clinical experience, I believe that reparenting is the key to recovery for the adult child. The messages we have received from dysfunctional parents, the defenses we have devised, and the resulting dislocation of healthy development have resulted in malfunctioning

[12]

adults. The protections we have learned to provide for ourselves are most often organized around survival issues. Indeed, they have served us well! We have survived, haven't we? And that power to survive is a strength that we can call on for recovery. But adult children, once grown up, are encumbered with excess baggage that no longer serves them. Weighted down, they are unable to proceed. Instead, they mark time in place or stagger backward, not knowing how to let go of the burdens of the past. However, the messages and behaviors that hinder adult children are "learned" messages and behaviors, and whatever we learn we can unlearn. We can replace old messages with other messages that serve us better. Reparenting is unlearning what does not serve us and replacing it with what enables us to develop our own greatest potential.

I have great respect for the unconscious mind. I think that our learning is edited and incorporated by that part of our brain, and that the unconscious mind can best be addressed through hypnosis. I also make use of stories as teaching tools during trance in the tradition of that great psychotherapist, Dr. Milton H. Erickson.

The idea of reparenting with stories told in trance developed gradually. The earliest trance story that I recall was told in 1979 to a young man I shall call Patrick. At that time he was almost 25 years old. Something about the way he presented himself evoked the image of a toddler first learning to stand upright. There was a kind of shaky uncertainty about him. One of his presenting problems was his inability to move out of his mother's house away from her criticism and demands. When we started to trance, a story emerged. It was a story about a very young child who wiggled and squirmed out of his mother's arms, slid to the floor, and crawled as fast as his short little legs could propel him to the nearest leg of his crib. When he reached it he proceeded to pull himself up hand over hand until he was almost perpendicular, with his fat little behind sticking out at an angle, and his sturdy short legs spread wide apart for balance. Looking back over his shoulder at his mother he smiled a triumphant drooling smile. Mother applauded and expressed encouragement and approval, whereupon he let go of the crib leg, stood swaying wildly for an instant and then fell kerplunk on his fat little behind. He looked at his mother with tears beginning to come, and opened his mouth wide to howl. But mother came and sat on the floor near him, making encouraging sounds of approval. So he decided to stop crying, turned his back on his mother, and started over again, hand over hand. Mother called father to come see what their fine son was learning to do. Father also expressed surprised approval. And that was the end of the story.

As I began to experiment with parenting stories told in trance, I observed that trance facilitated learning and change. When it became apparent to me that significant changes often followed the stories, I began to formulate a course of treatment that I call "reparenting" (with stories told in trance to adult children of dysfunctional families). The stories are always about "a mother" or "a father" or "a child," so that the client is free to identify with the characters in the story without feeling coerced. I say something like: the mother seems familiar . . . perhaps . . . yet . . . ; the baby is almost recognizable but . . . etc. I do not plan the stories. I never know when they will "tell themselves." I do know that they come directly from my unconscious, and that they are addressed to my clients' third ear, a reference to Nietzsche's phrase in *Beyond Good and Evil*.[5] It is with the third ear that we hear the metaphorical language of our intuition. The stories usually occur when my client is in a state of trance and I myself am in a somewhat altered state of consciousness.

You well may ask, "Why stories?" Stories are the source of all history as we know it, the oldest form of exchanging human knowledge and experience. Storytelling has been a vehicle for teaching since earliest history. It supplies a very important component of the socialization process, introducing and reinforcing cultural values. Stories are metaphors for our own experiences. We can fit them into the framework of our own lives, making sense of them as they would apply to us. We are able to accept what the story implies and to incorporate new messages more easily because they are presented as metaphors once removed; suggestion without command. In this way resistance need not be aroused.

I very carefully prepare my clients for trance. Adult children typically are slow to trust. Any change over which they think they might not have control meets with strong resistance. Even a slight hint of authoritative direction by the therapist can impede the course of therapy. On the other hand, their fear of rejection impels them to seem compliant and to behave in ways they think will please. By establishing rapport and lowering resistance, we can open the door for the unconscious to accept the metaphor of a story and to incorporate ideas for new possibilities.

So then, how can we establish the essential trusting relationship? I shall describe one way to prepare clients for hypnotherapy, which has proven to be the most successful way for me. Unlike Erickson, I never

[14]

start treatment with stories. Lacking his phenomenal skills, experience, and reputation, I need more time to establish rapport. My first step, like his, is to hear the client's story, noting vocabulary, body language, frames of reference, representational fields, story content, and the problems as they are perceived by the client. I also want to know about the other significant characters that people the client's life. While all this is taking place, I assume as closely as possible the client's physical posture and breathing rhythm. I also do a lot of affirmative head-nodding and "uh-huhs." At the end of the first session I say, briefly, that they must feel most uncomfortable (or unhappy, sad, angry, frustrated, stuck) and that I am glad they came in for treatment.

In the second session we review the clients' story briefly and talk about any new occurrences between sessions. Then I ask them what myths and suppositions they have heard about hypnosis before coming for treatment. I then answer any questions about the methods of hypnotherapy. I explain in general what happens, emphasizing that clients are always in charge, that their unconscious is protective and will bring them directly out of trance should they feel threatened in any way. I assure them that no one can persuade them in trance to do or think anything that is not in their own best interest or that would not be acceptable to them in full consciousness. As an example of the protective role of the unconscious, I say that they have probably experienced sleeping soundly at night undisturbed by accustomed noises. Garbage trucks can grind and squeal at 4 a.m., cans can bang, cats can fight, and they sleep on peacefully. However, let the slightest unusual noise occur—a window raised, or a stair tread creaking—and they are instantly wide awake and alert. It is their "protective witness" guarding their safety. The unconscious never sleeps and never relaxes its vigilance. I wind up this session by telling them that I plan to make a tape recording for them during our next session and that I will explain the purpose of the tape at that time.

The third session begins like the second sessions with a brief recap designed to reassure the client and to strengthen rapport. When clients appear to be at ease, I explain that I will use this session to make a tape especially for them. I add that I will explain its use and purpose when we have completed the tape, at which time they can decide if they want to make use of it. I consistently take great care to give them the power of decision.

In my office I have a bed-sized couch. I ask the clients to remove their shoes, generally make their clothing loose and comfortable, and

[15]

then lie down and pretend that they are going to bed for the night. I mention that it is OK to fall asleep, that we hear very well when we are asleep. Perhaps we incorporate what we hear even better than when awake. I ask if they have ever heard that one can learn a foreign language by listening to a tape while sleeping, and then I affirm that it is true. I begin recording, after suggesting that it would be better for them not to speak until I have finished since they will not want to hear their own voice on the tape. I always start out with the same message, adding only minor variations for particular needs.

"Lie down in your bed, relax, let the bed hold you up. Let go . . . and then let go again . . . and again. Concentrate on your breathing. Pretend there is a balloon right under your belly button. When you breathe in, the balloon fills WAY UP with air; when you breathe out, the balloon collapses almost all the way down to your spine. That is the natural way to breathe. That is the way babies and puppy dogs breathe. The natural way to breathe fills your lungs with good pure oxygen all the way to the very bottom and expels the carbon dioxide and other poisons all the way from the very bottom on out of your body. Just breathe slowly and naturally."

This technique is derived from Yogic breathing exercises, and I use it repetitively in subsequent sessions of trance induction. It is my first step in teaching concentration. I then proceed with detailed instruction, starting with the feet:

"Pay attention to your feet." (My voice has become cadenced with the client's breathing.) "Relax your heels; relax your insteps; relax the balls of your feet; relax each toe in turn; wiggle your toes a little; let go. Make your feet heavier and heavier." (With obese clients I substitute words like "limp" or "weightless.") I proceed in this detailed way up the body to the lower legs, the knees, the thighs, the pelvis, the genitals, the buttocks, the abdomen, the small of the back, the torso, the collarbone, the shoulders, upper arms, elbows, forearms, wrists, hands, thumbs, each finger in turn, saying, "Let go . . . then let go again." All of this is delivered in an even, monotonous, quiet tone in rhythm with the client's breathing.

I continue the tape with suggestions to relax the back of the neck, the scalp, the forehead, the eyelids (at which point many clients are in trance), the cheekbones, the jaw, the chin, the upper lip, the lower lip, the tongue. I conclude this part of the tape with, "Take your mind to any part of your body where you still feel tension . . . and deliberately let go . . . again . . . and again." Since the first part of the tape is designed to release tension and stress, one of the valuable side effects

[16]

is the relief of insomnia after hearing the tape each night for a month or so. Other benefits are the clinically demonstrable lowering of high blood pressure and the acceleration of healing. Of course, the primary purpose is to teach clients to focus their attention, the first step in trance induction. The soothing supportive cadence and the hypnotic rhythm of my speech induce tranquillity and the release of tension. Throughout the tape there is the inference of being taken care of, being supported, being cradled, which produces quiet pleasure and trust. At this point all but the most fearful or angry have become blissfully peaceful and relaxed.

In the second part of the tape, I talk about the great power at the command of our bodies and our minds: "Pay attention to your mind. You have a wonderful brain. In it are stored millions upon millions of facts that you have gathered through the years, even before you were born . . . all there for you, carefully catalogued, and available at an instant's notice, more efficient than the most sophisticated computer . . . a treasure store of resources . . . all there for you. You can summon even the most diverse facts at will, sort them out to form options, choose among your options to make decisions, and use your decisions to solve your problems. You can use your fine brain to solve your job problems, your family problems, your relationship problems, your love problems, your money problems . . . any problems you might have. Your brain is your problem-solving instrument. Use it to solve your problems. Don't ask your body to solve your problems. It doesn't know how. Your body knows how to perform at maximum efficiency, to keep itself well, and to heal itself when needed. It doesn't know how to solve your love problems, your money problems" (etc., etc., depending on each client's frame of reference). "Solve your problems with your fine brain and give your body permission to do what it knows how to do."

For a client with heart dysfunction or hypertension, I go into detail. For example, "Pay attention to your heart. Notice how steadily, faithfully it beats, slow, strong, steady, never stopping day or night, waking or sleeping, faithfully pumping the rich, life-giving blood throughout your system, and it has done so since before you were born. It knows how to perform efficiently, to keep itself well, and to mend itself if need be. Don't ask it to solve your problems, it doesn't know how. Solve your problems with your fine brain and give your heart permission to do what it knows how to do."

For respiratory dysfunctions, I translate the same message as it applies to bringing clean oxygen into the lungs and expelling poisons

"And now . . . you turn, and you may notice a large banquet table. It is covered with an elegant embroidered banquet cloth, and on it you might see gleaming silver, sparkling crystal, and shining china. Perhaps there are platters, on platters, on platters of all your favorite foods; and perhaps there are pitchers, and carafes of all your favorite beverages. Now you can approach and begin to select, first this delicacy and then that . . . taking your time . . . perhaps you sip, first this drink and then that . . . taking your time, chewing slowly, paying attention to flavor . . . and texture, before you swallow and feel it settle comfortably in your stomach. Now you can continue, asking yourself from time to time if you are still hungry or if you have had enough. If you wish to pay attention, your stomach can tell you when you have had enough. If your stomach tells you that you have had enough, you can turn away happily, knowing you may return whenever you feel hungry or thirsty. It is all here for you. Welcome to the world of tasting, eating, and drinking. You belong here, take your place in it. Welcome to the world!

"And now you may begin a slow, graceful dance. You might glide, and you might sway, you can reach and you can kneel, you may turn, and you may skip, and your dance can begin to grow faster and faster until you may leap and whirl in an exhilaration of movement and vitality. You can enjoy your grace and vigor. Welcome to the world of movement and dance. You belong here. Now you can take your place in the world of movement and dance. Welcome to the world. You belong here just like the flowers, and the birds, the sky, and the earth, the sun, the moon, the stars, and the clouds, the trees and the water! You, too, belong here. Welcome to the world! Welcome to the world!"

After a pause, I say, "In a little while I shall count to three. If this be daytime, when you hear the count of three, you might stretch, yawn, and at your own pace, taking your time, you can sit up, and when you . . . OPEN YOUR EYES[6] . . . you can feel relaxed, rested, full of well-being . . . you might feel energized, looking forward eagerly to whatever you have planned for the rest of the day. If this be nighttime, when you hear 'three,' you can reach over, flip off your tape recorder, snuggle under the covers, and fall into a deep restful sleep. You can awaken at the time you have set for yourself, and when you awaken you might stretch, perhaps yawn, and taking your time, at your own pace, you can sit up. When you open your eyes you will feel wonderfully rested and relaxed, full of well-being and vitality. You can look forward to making your day the most creative, productive, and enjoyable in your life so far. One ... two ... three." This concludes the tape.

When the client has listened to the tape every night for a while, commonly there is a marked decrease in tension and a marked increase in rapport between us. Our work together is enhanced and accelerated. Also, the sound of my voice often becomes a cue for the client to go into trance. In the following sessions, I induce trance, aiming for enhanced imagery and for deeper trance states. In the sense that I use it, imagery includes more than visualization. The tape includes all the senses: smell, taste, sight hearing, and kinesthetic feeling. I include emotions as well. I am careful not to be specifically descriptive, because the images a client summons from within are the most powerful. They are assembled from personal experience, memories, fantasies, and hopes I might say, "You can go to a favorite place," but I do not name a place or specify what will be encountered there. Erickson used such phrases as, "Perhaps you will, you might, you can, possibly," etc. His avoidance of direct command opened up possibilities for his patient, tapped the patient's own resources, and sidestepped possible resistance.

Sooner or later, in the course of treatment, a story begins to "tell itself." Most often, there seems to be no significant reaction to the story in that session. Sometimes as many as two or three sessions take place before the client comments on the story or alludes to some part of it; sometimes it is never mentioned at all. What is first noticeable is an evident change, a new plan, a new attitude, or an aura of hopefulness and new resolve. From that point unti termination, we work to implement and reinforce the changes.

After the "nursery" story I told to Patrick, I began to record my "parenting" stories as they occurred. The sequence was not chronological in the beginning, but as I noted the effectiveness of some of the sequences I began to organize them into a course of treatment for new clients. The stories or episodes included in this book are composites of recorded tapes of stories told to many clients. The detail varies from client to client according to their idiosyncratic needs, but the parenting framework is the same for every adult child. The stories begin before birth and progress through childbirth, then through the autistic, symbiotic, separation/individuation, oedipal, latency, puberty, and adolescent phases of human psychological development. There are some episodes that are more pertinent to female children, and some that are more pertinent to male children, but by and large they are interchangeable.

At this point, I would like to summarize what I believe to be the essential ingredients for the effective use of storytelling in reparenting.

First of all, I make careful, thoughtful preparations to establish rapport before I begin actual storytelling. I believe that rapport, however we establish it, is the magic "key" to the effective use of metaphor. Rapport makes the metaphor available to the client. In turn, the metaphor is powerful because it defuses resistance, in that a story is "once removed" so that the new possibilities it offers become intriguing suggestions rather than commands.

The stories begin spontaneously in the treatment sessions without previous conscious planning. Whenever I hear myself say, "I am going to tell you a story," it is the signal for me to flip on my tape recorder. The language of my unconscious proves to be quite child-like, which is, I believe, an important component of the therapeutic effectiveness of these reparenting stories. Once I had a fine teacher who said, "If you want to be heard when you teach, then speak as if addressing an eight-year-old."

It is important to bear in mind that the stories are *spoken* words; they must be read aloud, with our conscious minds on "hold." It is best to read one story at a sitting. I tell them to my clients one at a time at intervals of at least one week. I often repeat a story, sometimes several times, with variations according to perceived need. Occasionally I go back to a story if more work in that area is indicated. I always repeat the infancy stories, especially those in the preverbal periods, in order to make sure to establish a total sense of security so often lacking in infancy.

In brief, the stories are instructions to the unconscious, and they produce a simple gestalt: no excitement, no plot, no conflict, no moral dilemma . . . simple, and therefore uninteresting to the problem-solving conscious mind. In fact, life in the nursery *is* often boring. The simple, the good, the nurturing can be boring to the conscious mind in the same way that learning another language can be stultifyingly dull to an adult beginner. New parents are often boring as well, except to other new parents, and maybe even to them (perhaps they tolerate each other because only they can tolerate each other).

It is equally important to bear in mind that these stories are addressed to "adult children" who have been traumatized, and whose negotiation of developmental phases has been dislocated. They serve as templates for what should have happened in their actual experience to enable their developmental processes to proceed without a hitch. The unconscious mind seems to respond to the stories with, "Yes! Having finally experienced *this*, I can now get on with my *new* task!" The client gets beyond an impasse and can initiate a new life pattern. What is made available is the step that precedes reframing. If we ask what is the step before reframing, then the obvious answer must be framing, of course. Let us hypothesize that there have never been frames for developmental stages. How would we build them? Simply and gently, with undiluted goodness. We must concede also that, were the stories interesting to the conscious mind, they would have to contain inimical material (conflict, dilemmas, problems) that might do harm to the formation of the construct emerging in the unconscious mind of the client.

It will not escape notice that the context for these stories is predominately white and middle-class. Therapists could, therefore, use some judgment in changing the contexts to suit the needs of clients from other segments of society. Likewise, it will no doubt be noticed that traditional gender roles have been emphasized. Again, the judgment of the therapist could prevail in changing these role contents where essential. It is, of course, my belief that it should rarely be essential. There exists support in the literature for my contention that traditional gender roles facilitate favorable development. For further argument along these lines, the therapist may want to refer to works in which gender roles are more extensively discussed.[7]

The family in the stories is so idealized as to be unbelievable to the conscious mind. Mother and father behave in ways that would be highly improbable in a real-life family. However, clinically this vision of child-rearing seems to satisfy the unfulfilled longings of the unconscious mind. We must remember that the stories are not designed to teach parents how to parent, but rather to give new messages that make it possible for "adult children" to accept themselves as adequate and lovable, to give them permission to trust, to be spontaneous, and to love.

In addition to reparenting sessions, I offer weekly group sessions, which I facilitate. The supportive interaction among the adult children in groups definitely accelerates and reinforces change. For those clients who come from alcoholic families I often suggest ACOA meetings and other groups for codependents. However, my own groups do not follow the AA format. They are designed to reinforce reparenting messages. These messages are the messages all of us needed to receive from our parents; but very few of us were so fortunate. It was not necessarily true that they didn't love us, but most likely that they themselves never got good parenting messages from their own parents, and so on and on back through the generations. Now it is possible to stop the endless repetition of dysfunctional parenting. We can erase the bad messages and supply and reinforce good parenting messages. Of course, I do not mean to imply that reparenting is accomplished by the stories alone. They act as a kind of "open sesame" for other therapeutic factors of treatment to enter—factors which develop and reinforce healthy choices and changes.

Last of all, I am convinced that effective therapy through storytelling depends on the therapist's willingness to trust his or her own creativity and intuition, a willingness to open the self up to one's own unconscious and to allow it to take over. When we trust our unconscious, then our creativity flowers and proliferates. The books and tapes about Milton Erickson's anecdotes are a metaphor for our own inventiveness. It is not enough to offer pallid imitations of his stories, but rather to use his teachings as a springboard to catapult us into our own creativity. I hope that these stories will encourage other therapists to tell their own reparenting stories in their own way to adult children of dysfunctional families.

NOTES

[1]Mead, M. (1972). *Blackberry winter,* pp. 1–3. New York: William Morrow.

[2]Mead, M. (1978). *Culture and commitment,* p. 84. New York: Anchor Press/ Doubleday.

[3]Black, C. (1985). *Repeat after me.* MAC Pub.

[4]There was never alcohol of any kind in my parents' house. Neither of them ever drank alcohol. They had no need of alcohol to act "crazy." They were "crazy" enough without it.

[5]Nietzsche, F.W. (1886). *Beyond good and evil,* VIII:246, pp. 180–181. New York: Carlton House.

[6]This is an embedded message incorporated in a sentence and annotated by an increase in volume and a slight pause before and after, which I often use to bring a client out of trance.

[24]

[7]Readings about gender roles might include:

Lamb, M.E. (1981). Historical perspective on the father's role. In *The role of the father in child development* (2nd ed.). New York: Wiley.

Maccoby, E., & Jacklin, C. (1974). *The psychology of sex differences.* Stanford: Stanford University Press.

Mahler, M.S., Pine, F., & Bergman, A. (1975). *The psychological birth of the human infant.* New York: Basic Books

Stevens, J.H., & Mathews, M. (Eds.). (1978). *Mother/child, father/child relationships.* Washington, DC: The National Association for the Education of Young Children.

AUTHOR'S NOTE: To those who may imagine that they recognize themselves or others in the following stories: The names and sometimes the gender of the clients in the following stories have been changed to preserve professional confidentiality. All the stories have been told to more than one client, and so the characters who appear in them are not particular persons but a composite of several people.

Because I find it awkward to write he/she I have chosen to arbitrarily assign gender throughout. In most of the stories gender can be exchanged at will, and in practice I do so freely whenever it is appropriate.

Normal Autistic Phase

Pregnancy

This is a story about a young woman. She is leaning forward eagerly in the doctor's office, never taking her eyes off his face as he says to her, "Well, my dear, congratulations. Your dearest wish is being fulfilled." She says not a word, but holds her breath and watches his face. He says, "You are pregnant," whereupon her whole body relaxes.

A wonderful, angelic smile spreads over her face, and she whispers, "Are you sure?"

"Completely sure, there is no doubt of any kind. You are now, I'd say, let me see, probably six or seven weeks pregnant."

"Oh, doctor, thank you so much."

He leans back in his chair and laughs out loud. Then he says, "I didn't do it. You did."

She laughs and says, "Oh, I'm so excited! Oh, I just can't wait to tell my husband."

Pointing, he says, "The phone's right there."

She looks at him, uncertainly, and then she says, "Well, OK." She dials her husband's number. When he answers, she says, "I am, I am, it's true, it's true." We can't hear what he says, but she smiles all over when he says it, and then she says, "OK, darling, 6 o'clock?" She hangs up.

The doctor is beaming. He stands, indicating that it is time for her to usher herself out. She rises and walks over to him. "May I give you a hug?" He holds out his arms and she hugs him, tells him how happy she is, and leaves his office.

And that is the end of the first part of this story.

The next part is about the same young woman. She is sitting in a rocking chair in her own household. She is wearing a loose housecoat, and she is very, very pregnant. Her husband stands near the doorway saying to her, "Are you sure you're all right?"

"Of course I'm all right," she responds irritably.

"Well, you said that you thought you were having contractions, darling, about five minutes ago."

"I know, I know, but I'm sure it can't be that. Can it, do you think it is?"

"It could be, it's sort of in the time slot that the doctor said."

"Oh, darling, isn't it exciting! I can't wait! Do you think, maybe, do you think we ought to go to the hospital?"

"I don't know, I think I'll call the doctor."

"OK, call the doctor, go on, call the doctor, hurry, hurry."

He leaves the room and calls the doctor. After a long wait that seems like forever, while the young woman is tapping her foot and impatiently looking at her watch, but at the same time so very excited, he finally comes back and reports, "The doctor said . . . "

"Yes, yes, hurry, what did he say?"

"He said to relax and to start timing the contractions."

"What contractions?"

"Honey, you said a little while ago that you had contractions."

"Oh, who knows what kind of contractions those were. Who knows? Probably gas."

The young man shrugs his shoulders and says, "Would you like something to eat?"

"EAT? Who can eat at a time like this?"

"OK," he says, "I think I'll fix myself something."

"Well, go ahead, if you can eat. I don't see how anybody can eat at a time like this." He turns away silently and walks down the hall shaking his head. He goes into the kitchen, and starts making a sandwich. As he's toasting the bread, he hears a voice behind him. He turns to find her looking at him accusingly. "You really are going to eat, aren't you?"

Silence. Then he asks, "Well, have you been timing?"

"Of course not, I feel fine."

"OK, then how about me fixing you something to eat?"

"Oh well, yes, if you insist." He makes another sandwich and they sit down together. She smiles at him sheepishly, and says, "I am being impossible, am I not?"

"Mumhum," he says, with his mouth full. She begins to eat.

[30]

Just as she is finishing, she looks at him. Her eyes get very big, and she gasps, "OOOOH, that was a real one."

Startled, he asks, "What, what was a real one?"

She replies, "A contraction!" She sits rigidly fixing her attention on her watch.

He gets up, and starts clearing the table, saying, "Do you think maybe you could dry the dishes while you're waiting for your next contraction?"

"How can you expect me to do something like that in my condition?"

"Oh, honey, OK, OK, just make yourself comfortable and watch the clock."

Some 20 minutes later she exclaims, "There's another one! Call the doctor! Call the doctor right away! Do you think we have time to get to the hospital?"

He dials the doctor's number, and he tells the doctor that she had two contractions, and they were 20 minutes apart. There's a long pause, and he says, "All right, sir, I'm sorry sir, yes, sir, yes, yes, I will, OK, goodbye, sir." He turns around, and says, "We're not to call him until the contractions are five minutes apart."

"FIVE MINUTES APART, it will take us at least 10 minutes to get to the hospital. I'll have the baby in the car!"

"OK, we'll cheat a little and call him when they're 10 minutes apart, and tell him they're five minutes apart, all right?"

"What kind of a doctor do we have that we have to lie to him?" she exclaims, starting to cry.

"Honey," putting his arm around her, "Could you relax? Let's go into the other room and watch television."

"TELEVISION, NOW? I might miss a contraction!"

"Honey, I don't think you're going to miss any contractions. Come, let me help you."

She gets up awkwardly, and staggers, balancing her swollen belly. Walking with her legs slightly apart, she waddles into the next room. "Oh, isn't this exciting? Do you think maybe the baby will come tonight?"

"Maybe."

So they watch television, and soon she's fast asleep. He covers her, and lowers the recliner chair gently. Suddenly she sits bolt upright, "Uuuuhhhhh, what time is it?"

"Well, this one is, I think, about 10 minutes after the other."

[31]

"Oh, get the suitcase, get the suitcase." He runs for the suitcase. She says, "Let's go, hurry, hurry, I know the baby is coming, the baby is coming." They scramble into the car.

As he drives at breakneck speed, he says, "If a cop picks me up now, what am I going to say?"

"You'll tell him to escort us, that a baby is on the way!"

"OK, honey." But no police intercept them, and soon they arrive at the hospital. The young husband rushes in. His hair is sticking up in all directions, his tie is undone, he looks frantic. She comes waddling after him, looking like a madonna, calm, beatific, with her eyes wide, innocent and full of dreams.

As they come to the counter, the nurse in the emergency room asks, "What is it? What's the trouble?"

He shouts, "Hurry, hurry, her contractions are 10 minutes apart."

The nurse looks at him down her nose, and says to his young wife, "Come this way. We'll put you in a wheelchair, dear, and take you upstairs to your room. Who is your doctor? We'll call him."

"Ooooh, I don't think there's time for him to come," she moans.

The nurse replies, "I think there's time. I think there's lots of time. So we'll get you upstairs." And over her shoulder she says to the young husband, "Do you think you can manage to sit there in the waiting room and relax?"

He looks at her sheepishly, and says, "Yes, ma'am."

Then they go upstairs, and that's the end of the episode.

Fetus in Uterus

You are in a three-dimensional space, inside of a more or less round space. You seem to be floating in there, in a marvelous body-temperature fluid, and you touch the sides, which are soft and resilient, something like foam rubber. You touch the sides occasionally, then float, and sometimes you seem to be floating upside down and sometimes right side up and sometimes sideways, but always slowly, comfortably, almost soundlessly in the most soothing kind of rhythmic turning and floating. And somewhere in the space there is a muffled sound almost like a soft drumbeat: BOOM, boom, BOOM, boom, BOOM, a beautifully comforting and soothing and rhythmic drumbeat, and you seem somehow to be turning, and somehow moving to the rhythm of the drum. Sometimes you seem to experience turbulence, and you feel yourself becoming more active, almost agitated, and you kick out with your feet, and even thrust out with your fists, and sometimes butt with your head, and then the turbulence subsides and you're again aware of BOOM, boom, BOOM, and you are immersed, surrounded and safe as though enclosed in a soft floating balloon. You still hear the drumbeat. You are quietly floating. You are floating in a kind of underwater world, warm and peaceful, and still the only sound is the sound of the distant drum. It is wonderful. Now and then you feel a rush of energy, mysterious stimulation, and sometimes it causes you to move your arms and legs vigorously, and then it subsides. Sometimes there seems to be a foreign substance that comes into you and causes you to behave erratically and that lasts for a little while and then it subsides.

Now something begins to happen that is very different. The walls of this beautiful cavern begin to undulate and they come closer and then they expand, and then they come closer, and then they expand, and you are caught up in that rhythm. Your body turns and turns until you are head down. You start to push when the walls come close and to let go when they recede and push and let go and all the time there is the BOOM, boom, BOOM, boom, BOOM, boom, push and let go, push and let go. Walls come close and walls expand and undulate and you are pushed and you push and now you don't know whether you are pushing or you are pushed. And it's all a marvelous reciprocal rhythm that goes completely in time with the drumbeat. And as you push down with your head, the pressure grows greater and you strain more and the intervals get smaller until it's one long prolonged squeeze of the walls and push of you.

Suddenly, you seem to shoot into another space. You feel yourself grasped firmly and held up. And you hear a loud . . . it seems to come from you . . . a long wail of a cry, and then you are softly wrapped, and as you cry, cold air comes into your lungs for the first time and bright lights assault your eyes, and then you are gently laid down. You feel soft arms embrace you, holding you firmly, and you are held against soft skin, your skin against skin. The wrapping is loosened gently and quietly and you hear a voice murmuring softly, a lovely voice that quiets you and quiets you.

And then you hear the voice say, "I have to see. Oh, yes, I have to see. Oh yes, it is a little girl. Oh, I am so happy. Let me count her toes." And gently each toe is touched and wiggled. And, "Let me count her fingers. Oh, how tiny, how perfect, how beautiful she is!" You feel yourself wrapped and held gently, skin against skin.

And she who is holding you is now talking to another standing near, and his voice is deep and also gentle and soft. He's saying, "No, I don't think she's that beautiful, she looks sort of red and wrinkled to me."

And the other voice says, "Oh, you, you always tease. She's the most beautiful thing in the world and you know it."

And then there is laughter and teasing and he asks if he can hold his little daughter. They talk about names. Gently he takes her and holds her for a few moments and then carefully puts her back down in her mother's arms.

And that is the end of this episode.

Birth

This episode takes place in the delivery room, and the young woman has just given birth. The doctor catches the baby, and as the nurse takes it from him, it wails loudly, and the young mother says, "Ooh, bless its heart! Listen to it!"

And the doctor says, "Bless YOUR heart. You did fine." Then he says, "You have a fine baby girl."

Her eyes close, and she smiles all over her face. She says softly, "Isn't that lovely." The nurse cleans the baby, and puts her in her mommy's arms. She holds her and cuddles her. Then she undoes the swaddling, and examines her baby carefully. She counts her toes and then she counts her fingers, and then she looks down to be sure she is a girl. Then she says, "Yes, it's a girl," and she holds her baby close. Her husband comes into the room and she says, "Oh, honey, isn't it wonderful. Look at her, isn't she darling?"

He leans over and looks intently at his daughter, "Mmm, yeah, pretty darling."

And she says, "You don't think she's darling?"

"I didn't say she isn't darling."

"You did too."

"I do think she's darling . . . what do you want me to say? She's kinda red, and she's pretty wrinkled."

"She is not, she's beautiful!"

"OK, honey, she's beautiful, and I love you, and I'm very proud."

"Ooooh, I'm so tired, I think I'll sleep now."

The nurse takes the baby from her, and the young mother falls asleep instantly.

And that's the end of the story.

Newborn

The tenderly smiling mother sits in the rocker looking down at her baby whose little form is molded against hers. Her small fist, her pink curled fist, is tightly grasping her mother's forefinger, the tiny fingers almost encircling it. The little baby is placidly sleeping, completely relaxed in mother's cuddling arms.

Now the baby stirs and makes rooting and nudging movements with her head like a little billy goat butting gently against her mother's body. Mother smiles with pleasure, reaches down and uncovers her breast, helping baby find the nipple. She keeps on searching and rooting and nudging until finally mother presses the nipple into her baby's rosebud mouth, but the little mouth is inexperienced with sucking. She sucks a few times and loses the nipple again. Mother helps again, and this happens repeatedly. Finally the baby seems to catch on, and sucks vigorously. Mother's body relaxes and she holds her tenderly, as she looks down into the little face sucking the milk hungrily. And when baby lets go of the nipple from time to time and loses it, her little lips are parted and milk spills out. Mother smiles and puts the nipple back as she presses baby's rosy face against her skin. Mother and baby are one, baby and mother are one, and mother is rocking gently. Under her breath she is singing a little song that goes, "Loo loo loo loo loo loo loo bye bye, up in . . . arms . . . soon you'll be asleepin'." Now baby's eyes are closed. Her lips part and stop sucking, and she is fast asleep.

Her mommy takes her over to the diapering table and gently, gently, tenderly, tenderly lays her down, keeping a hand on her all the time, easing her head down softly on the table, and then still holding, she removes the little soiled diaper with one hand and drops it into the pail. Gently and tenderly she washes her little daughter's bottom, carefully dries all the small fat creases. Smiling, she rediapers her, folds her wrapper around her securely, and stands looking down into her face. Baby opens her eyes. They are lovely gray-blue. Mommy tries to catch her look, to make eye contact, but baby's eyes are vague. She doesn't seem to see her mother yet, although mother searches and looks and seeks her out.

Baby's eyes close again slowly and mommy picks her up in her arms and takes her over to her crib. There, she keeps her arm under her baby, firmly, all the way down to the mattress. She gently releases her, covers her tenderly with a little soft blanket. Mother watches for another few moments to see that she is comfortable and fast asleep, and then walks to the intercom, turns it on, and tiptoes out of the room, closing the door behind her.

Baby has a calm sleep, and when at last she stirs and utters her first cry, mother is already there beside her, murmuring, "There now, there now, mommy's here." She picks up her little daughter and holds her close.

And that's the end of this episode.

Newborn Bonding

This story is about a very, very young infant, a newborn infant, and it takes place in a bright, clean, cheerful room with a small crib, and a diapering table which is also a bath table, a playpen, and a rocker. Mother is sitting in the rocker, gentle, smiling, calm . . . a quite contented mother. In her arms she is holding her small infant tenderly. She has her arm firmly supporting him from the back of his head to where her hand cups his little buttocks, and her other hand is holding him so that his legs are secure, as she firmly presses him against her breast. His eyes are closed and she is looking lovingly down into his face. He stirs. His eyelids slowly open. His gaze is unfocused, vague. His little face is relaxed. Mommy looks into his eyes and tries to capture his gaze, but he seems to be still within his own world. Still, he is content to be held against his mommy's warm skin which he feels next to his cheek, content with the smell of his mother, content with hearing her humming voice, content just to continue to be a part of her. He is not yet aware of himself as separate in any way. And mommy, too, experiences him as a very important part of herself as she looks at him and he seems to look back at her. She can't tell if he sees her or not, but she is intrigued and cannot take her eyes off his face. She smiles at him as she sings and rocks.

Then he begins to move his head. He turns his head toward her and begins, like a little piggy, to root against her breast. His mouth is seeking as he turns. She helps him and guides him to the nipple. He starts to feed, eagerly slurping, grunting, letting go to gasp, letting the milk run out of his greedy mouth, and then nursing again like a suckling pig.

Oh, oh, now his little face screws up as he lets go of the nipple, pulls his knees up to his belly and squirms in his mommy's arms. She says, "Uh oh, I see we have a bubble," lifting him up gently and laying him upright against her shoulder. She pats his little back and rubs it and rubs it and pats it until, finally, out comes a large belch. Mommy holds him away from her, looks at him and says, "Oh what a fine sturdy boy you are, that was wonderful," as she lowers him down again in her arms.

And again he roots and butts and finds the nipple and nurses greedily until his eyelids begin to get heavy and heavier and heavier. Finally he lets go of the nipple and sleeps with his little lips slightly parted. Mommy looks down at him fondly, leans over and nuzzles the fuzz on the top of his head. She sniffs him with delight and then she gently gets up, walks over to the crib, and ever so tenderly leans over until his body touches the sheet, and only then does she release her firm grasp. She covers him softly, turns on the intercom, and tiptoes out of the room.

And that is the end of this episode.

Bath Time

This is about a very, very young infant. You see a beautiful room, bright, cheerful, clean, and you can tell that it's a baby's room, a nursery. There's a crib with a mobile hanging above it and the parts of the mobile turn brightly in all their primary colors, and move gently in the air. There's a rocker and a diapering table which is also a baby bath. There's a playpen, and in the crib sleeping quietly on his tummy is a very, very tiny newborn infant. His mommy is standing by the crib looking down at him with a little smile on her lips, watching his peaceful, even breathing and his quiet sleep. It seems as if she could stand there forever, watching her little son, who now stirs.

His fists quiver, rise up in the air a bit and come down on the sheet. His fat little legs make crawling movements, and as mommy watches, his eyes open. Then he opens his mouth wide to let out his first yell of discomfort. Mommy reaches down, grasps him firmly, supports his head, and turns him over gently. Then she lifts him up and holds him close against her shoulder so that his face touches the skin of her neck. She holds him firmly by his bottom and by the nape of his neck as well, to hold his wobbling head steady. Sensuously she sniffs the side of his downy head, and closes her eyes blissfully. Then she walks over to the bath table and firmly holds his little body as she lowers him onto the table.

Then gently and lovingly she removes his wrapper and drops it to the floor. She removes his socks and drops them on the wrapper, and then she undoes his diaper and drops it into the pail. Meanwhile baby is squawling at the top of his healthy lungs, and she is murmuring to him, "There, there, sweet darling, there there, my lovely baby, there

[40]

there, honey, there there." Then she lifts him up and uncovers the bath that is under the diaper platform. She puts her elbow in the water to make sure it's exactly the right temperature, and when she has satisfied herself that the water is just right, she lowers him, holding him firmly with her whole arm from elbow to wrist, down the length of his back. With her other hand she holds his body steady so that he feels supported and safe. Never does she allow him to feel as though he might fall. Then she slowly and carefully lowers him into the warm water. When he feels the water his cries subside. Soon they are only a little crooning, complaining murmur, "Mmmmmrrroooo-woooo." Mommy is crooning and talking to him all the time. Her voice quiets him.

Then carefully and slowly she sponges him. She bathes his chest with the softest of cloths. She cleans his little bottom, and she washes around his genitals. Then she carefully washes the insides of his thighs and down his legs. When she gets to his feet she washes each little toe, and cannot resist a kiss on each. Then she washes his arms, and under his arms, and his fingers one by one. Then gently she wipes his face with the washcloth, then his ears and behind his ears. Baby has gentled into a little croon, and a little coo, and then into quietness. His mommy turns him over, and again firmly holding his body, she washes his back. With her other hand she lifts a big fluffy towel and wraps him completely from head to toe. Lowering the top of the diapering table, she lays him gently on the table, and ever so carefully dries him. She towels his head dry, towels his face and body, making sure that she dries all the sweet little creases, all the plump little rolls. She tends to each finger and to each toe.

When she has finished she lifts and kisses the bottom of his foot. Putting his foot down she says, "This little piggy went to market," and she wiggles his big toe. "And this little piggy stayed home. This little piggy had roast beef, and this little piggy had none, and this little piggy cried 'wee wee wee wee wee' all the way home." All of this is for her own pleasure, of course, because baby is too little to know what is going on. But this he knows: he knows his mother's firm warm touch, he knows the feel of her skin against his skin, he knows the complete comfort of being safely, firmly nestled in her embrace.

Now wonderfully comfortable after his bath, he begins to feel hungry, and he lets out a mighty yell. Mommy quickly puts a clean diaper on him, and a wrapper, and clean socks, and then a little blanket all around him to keep him warm. Holding him cradled in her arms against her body, she moves to the rocking chair. She carefully

[41]

sits down with him, takes one breast from the front of her dress and holds her nipple to his little squawling mouth. He instantly stops in the middle of a yell, and nuzzling like a little animal, he finds her nipple. Strong, strong, he pulls and sucks, as his body begins to relax in her arms. She looks down at him lovingly. His unseeing slate-blue eyes look up into hers. And who knows if he sees or he doesn't? But he sucks and gurgles and drools milk: an eager little piggy, utterly content. His mommy watches him, looking into his eyes and wondering what he is feeling, what he is thinking. She watches for some reaction, unaware of the little smile that transforms her face as she looks at her beautiful little boy. When at last he has stopped gurgling, slurping, and sucking, she holds him up to her shoulder and with gentle pats on his back, she coaxes out a mighty belch, and then suckles him again, watching him, then burping him again, until finally his eyes begin to droop shut. Her eyes close and open sympathetically with his, until at last his eyelids stay shut and his rosy little mouth lets go of her nipple. A little milk dribbles out of the corner of his lips and he is fast asleep.

In a few moments his mommy gets up, walks to his crib, gently lays him down, covers him with his blanket, stands watching him for a few moments while she croons a lullaby, unaware that she is singing. Then with a smile on her face she flips on the intercom and quietly leaves the room, gently closing the door behind her.

And that is the end of this story.

First Smile

It's evident that this story takes place some time later, for baby seems a little larger and heavier. Mommy is standing by his crib and he is lying there squawling, waving his feet and hands in the air. His little face is red. Mommy leans over him saying, "There, there, darling, mommy's here, mommy's here." He opens his eyes as mommy picks him up and holds him close. She takes him over to the diapering table. There she deftly undoes his diaper and drops it in the pail. Then she gently washes him, carefully, in all his little fat creases, and then she diapers him again, fastens his little wrapper around him, and picks him up.

She goes over to the rocker and sits down with him. He is looking at her as she looks into his eyes. She thinks he is looking at her as she is looking at him and they look at each other for quite some time. Then a little smile comes across his face. "Oh," his mommy exclaims, "Oh, you're smiling! You smiled at me!" But the little smile is gone. She quickly runs to the door, and she calls, "Daddy, come here! He smiled, he just smiled at me!"

Daddy comes in and looks, and says, "I don't see any smile." They both stand and watch while she holds him. Suddenly baby smiles again and daddy says, "That's gas, he's not smiling. He just burped."

But mommy says, "How can you say that? That was a smile, I could tell."

"Well, I could call it a smile at me, if you like, and you could call it a smile at you, if you like, but I still say it's gas."

"Oh, you!"

He waves and says, "I'll see you later."

As he leaves, mommy sits down and watches, but baby is impatient and butts her as he reaches out for her. Mommy guides him to the nipple, and he nurses again. Together they enjoy this encounter, and as he nurses he never takes his eyes away from her eyes, and she never shifts her eyes from his. They sit entranced, enrapt in each other, as baby's eyes gaze calmly, sweetly, intently into his mother's face. Their eyes are locked together in a special communication, special wonderful eye contact that has secret meaning for both.

When baby again closes his eyes and sleeps, she continues to sit gazing into his face, remembering the little smile, and wondering if it really was just gas. Actually, he didn't seem to be smiling just at her. Still, she loves it, and keeps smiling to herself, remembering.

Finally, slowly, she gets up, and holding him firmly, carefully she puts him into the crib. Then she notices that one of his little hands is still curled around one of her fingers. She has been so busy gazing into his eyes and watching for his smile that she was not aware that he was holding her finger tightly in his little pink fist. Gently, ever so gently, stroking his hand, she releases her finger, tucks his hand under the warm cover, turns on the intercom, and tiptoes out of the room.

And that is the end of this episode.

Normal Symbiotic Phase

Baby Makes Eye Contact

This story begins with what looks like a beautiful baby's room, a nursery, and in it is a crib, and a rocker. Mommy is sitting in the rocker. There is a playpen, and a diaper table that is also a bath. A little baby is just stirring in her crib after a long nap. As she stirs, her mommy is already there, leaning over the crib, looking into her baby's sweet face, and smiling in anticipation. This baby seems very familiar to you, and so does her mommy. Baby opens her eyes, and mommy's face changes expression with surprise and delight, for baby looks straight into her eyes, and as mommy looks back, she thinks she perceives a little smile, and that baby's eyes have focused and have really seen her. Mommy is delighted. She leans over again and tries to make eye contact. But baby's attention has wandered now, and daddy says, "I don't see her focusing on anything."

"Oh just wait, just wait. That was so exciting! She looked right into my eyes. Just wait. And she smiled, I swear it."

"Darling, you know that was probably gas."

"Oh, you! You just really don't want to believe. This is a wonderful kid. She can do everything. She's just so smart! She did make eye contact with me, and she did smile."

"OK, OK, have it your way, have it your way. I'm sure in good time she will be able to make contact and smile so we both can see it. Until then, I have to go back to my work." And daddy leaves the room.

Mommy picks up her dear little baby, and holds her close to her heart. Baby squirms a little, and mommy walks over to the diaper table, undresses her tenderly, undoes her diaper, drops it in the pail, sponges her, then she lifts her up, careful to support her head and her back. Baby seems to mold to mommy's body as she holds her. She is almost clinging, and in fact, her fat little hand has twined around her mother's forefinger, and is holding on tight, grasping it with surprising strength. Mommy uncovers the bath which she has already prepared, adds a little hot water, and then dips her bare elbow into it, testing to see if it's the right temperature. And, still holding baby firmly, supporting her head and her back, and cupping the little buttocks in her hand, she lowers her slowly into the water and gently, gently holds her as she slips her arm away. Baby looks around and waves her arms and feet, obviously enjoying what is happening. Mommy takes a sponge and soap and carefully, carefully bathes her. When she is all washed and rinsed, mommy picks her up in one swift movement and wraps her from head to toe in a warm towel. She encases the little round head in the towel, letting the small face peek out. Then she takes her over to the rocker, and there in her lap, systematically and carefully, dries her all over.

Baby is squirming and kicking and moving, and mommy says, "Yes, yes, my darling, I know you're hungry. Just a minute darling. Yes, you're going to get fed very soon, lovey." Mommy discards the damp towel, reaches for a blanket, and wraps her darling snugly in it. Then she gets up, takes her to the diaper table, and puts a clean diaper on her, and then a little flannel wrapper, which she ties in a secure bow around her middle. Then she takes her back, gently, gently to the rocker. Sitting in the rocker, she takes one breast out of the front of her dress, takes her baby's face and directs it toward the nipple. Baby gropes, pushes, nuzzles, and butts her mommy like a small goat. At last she connects with the nipple and begins strong sucking. Mommy relaxes, and looks fondly at her little girl child.

The two sit completely joined, completely together, feeling like one, like one person again, just as it was before birth. Mommy looks down tenderly, and baby looks up, and again mommy is surprised, delighted, enchanted. Baby is unmistakably making eye contact. Only for a few seconds, but still, recognition passes between them. Baby lets go of the nipple for a moment, just a moment, and a ghost of a smile appears again. And mommy thinks, "She knows me, she recognizes me."

Meanwhile baby has again eagerly started nursing, and is totally preoccupied. Suddenly a frown crosses her face, and her mouth opens to let out a squeal. Her little knees come up against her chest, and mommy says, "Oh, oh, oh, oh, have we got a bubble?" And she lifts her up, holding her against her shoulder, and pats her gently but vigorously on the back, bouncing her ever so slightly up and down.

[48]

Pretty soon, yes indeed, there comes a loud hearty belch, and mommy smiles with satisfaction saying, "Good, that was a big air bubble hurting my baby right in the middle." She lays baby down again, and baby starts nursing eagerly until she has her fill, while mommy patiently, adoringly watches, humming a little tune in her throat. She's humming a lullaby. And the lullaby is, "Loo loo loo loo loo loo loo loo bye bye, up in mommy's arms be creepin' and soon you'll be asleepin', singing loo loo loo loo loo loo loo loo, bye." Baby's eyes droop and close, and her small mouth slackens as a dribble of milk spills out the corner. She lets go of the nipple, and is fast asleep. Mommy puts her down in her crib on her tummy, just in case there are more air bubbles, and covers her with a soft blanket. She stands for a moment watching her darling sleep. Then she turns on the intercom, tiptoes quietly out of the room, and gently closes the door.

And that is the end of this story.

Baby Holds Head Up

This story is about a baby who seems very familiar to you. He is lying in his crib waving his hands and his feet and looking around with eyes that seem to be focusing. They seem to follow the movements of the mobile that hangs above his crib. They seem to follow the movement a little from side to side. Leaning over the crib is a young woman watching. She is smiling calmly. She looks into her baby's eyes and the baby seems to look back. She thinks she detects a little smile on the baby's face, but she's not sure. She reaches down and picks him up, holding his head, and supporting it with her hand. As the baby lies against her shoulder she gently takes her hand away, and the baby supports his head by himself. "Oh," she says, "How wonderful! He can hold his head up by himself!" And she goes quickly to the door, opens it and calls down the hall, "Daddy, daddy, come see what your fine baby boy can do. He can actually hold his head up by himself."

The baby's daddy comes down the hall smiling, looks at his son and says, "Well indeed he can. Isn't he a fine strong boy!" And they congratulate each other on how strong and fine their sturdy son is. Then daddy says, "Well, I must get back now. I'll peek in later."

Mommy waves as she sits down in the rocker. She holds her baby and talks to him a little. Then she gets up and puts him on his diapering table. She undoes his diaper, and drops it in the pail. She takes a soft cloth and warm water and she carefully wipes him off and cleans him up, and then she takes the softest of towels and she gently pats him dry. She puts a fresh diaper on him.

When he is all comfortable again she picks him up and takes him to the rocker. There she takes out one breast and he eagerly starts to nurse. "Oh, what a hungry little fellow," she says fondly, as he sucks vigorously. Every once in a while he looks up at her and catches her eye, and when he does he lets go of the nipple. The milk runs down his chin. Then quickly he grabs the nipple again earnestly, and seriously goes back to work. She smiles, almost laughing at him, while he nurses. As he nurses she hums a little song to him as she very gently rocks. She sings a little lullaby, and baby looks into her eyes, never stopping sucking, but with his eyes looking into hers. When he finally lets his eyes droop a little, he relaxes his mouth and gradually lets go of the nipple. Mommy sings to him. She sings, "Loo loo loo loo loo loo bye bye, and soon you'll be asleeping, singing loo loo loo loo loo loo bye." His eyes are shut now and his sweet face is relaxed. Mommy puts him back in his crib and covers him tenderly. Then she tiptoes out of the room after turning on the intercom so she can hear him the moment he awakens.

When he awakens and stirs in his crib and utters the first gurgling murmur, mommy swiftly enters the room again and stands by his crib. When he opens his eyes, she is standing there smiling at him. He waves his hands and kicks his feet and mommy picks him up and holds him close.

And that is the end of this episode.

Eye Contact and Smiles

This is a story about a little baby. This baby is no longer new-born. He has grown some, but he still looks familiar, as does his mommy. The scene is in the same nursery with the same furnishings. Mommy is bending down over the crib, and baby is looking up into her face. There is unmistakable eye contact as baby looks into mommy's face and mommy looks into baby's face. Mommy is talking and baby's eyes are wide open looking straight at his mother, then suddenly, in response to mother's smile, a beautiful big, loose, wet smile appears on baby's face.

Mommy is enchanted and calls her husband who comes unhurriedly down the hall looking resigned. "Now what?"

And she says, "Well, just come and see now, you just come and see!" She pulls him over to the crib and looks down at her baby. Baby looks back into her eyes. Mommy puts her finger just under baby's chin and strokes it, and baby gives her the biggest, wettest, toothless smile you have ever seen.

Daddy exclaims, "Well, I'll be . . . he really is looking at you and he is smiling!" At the sound of his voice and the movement of his face near him, baby looks at him and turns his face towards him. "Look, he's looking at my eyes! He can see my eyes! He's looking at me!"

His wife reaches over and gives him a little squeeze as he continues, "Look at him smile at his daddy!"

And mommy says, "You see! You see!"

Daddy reaches down and picks up a rattle. As he shakes it, baby's eyes follow the rattle. He kicks his feet and beats his hands, and goos and coos.

[52]

"Listen to that!" mommy exclaims, "Listen to that!"

Daddy is smiling delightedly. He holds the rattle closer to baby. It makes a noise. Baby looks at it, startled, and it makes another noise. He watches it, fascinated. He is full of curiosity. 'Isn't he the most intelligent baby you ever saw in your whole life? Look, he knows about the rattle.'

Her husband looks at her skeptically, "He doesn't know about the rattle. The rattle makes a noise so he looks at it. I don't think he knows what's making the rattle make a noise."

"Oh, you! I think he does!" And they both continue to watch, fascinated, as daddy shakes the rattle, and baby looks at it, and looks at mommy, and looks at daddy, and then looks around, and smiles out into the world.

Then she leans over and picks up her little son, holding him firmly. This time she doesn't have to support his head. Baby is holding his head upright against mommy's shoulder. Then he begins to make crawling motions on her shoulder, and mommy says, "OK, honey, OK. We'll tend to you now."

And mommy takes him to the diapering table to change him, while he kicks and squirms, and keeps on smiling indiscriminately into the air. She is talking to him, and when she talks his eyes move to hers and he looks into her eyes. She is saying nonsense things to him. "What a cute little honey bear, what a sweet little darling, what a good little fellow." And he is watching her moving face with his big eyes, completely entranced.

Then she carries him back to the rocker for his feeding. Baby is still holding the rattle, and still looking at it with astonishment whenever he moves. This time, he doesn't root for the for the nipple like a blind little piglet. This time he finds the nipple and placidly sucks as mommy looks down tenderly.

Daddy is watching with a little smile on his face too. Pretty soon he tiptoes out.

Mommy sits watching and humming to her baby. Baby fixes his eyes on his mother's eyes as she nurses him. They seemed joined together by the gaze between them, mother to baby, baby to mother. Mother is smiling and baby lets go of the nipple to smile a big milky smile in response. The milk runs out of the corner of his mouth. Mommy laughs out loud with delight. Baby smiles again, all the time looking into mommy's eyes. Then he turns and finds the nipple, still looking out of the corner of his eyes at her. It seems very clear that he knows his mommy, smiles at her, and recognizes her face. Together they are joined in a long embrace of gazing into each other's eyes. Joined.

When baby has stopped nursing, mommy puts him down on his tummy on a blanket on the floor, and says, "Now, darling, if you have a big air bubble, this will help it come up." Sure enough, here it is, a loud belch, and mommy pats him on his little diapered behind.

Then she sits down beside him and puts the rattle where he can reach it. Baby touches it, and it makes a noise. And again baby's eyes look at it with astonishment, but he doesn't reach for the rattle and doesn't seem to make a connection between grasping it with his hand and the noises that the rattle makes.

Then, she thinks he may have another bubble, so she props him upright against her shoulder. Whereupon he digs his little feet into her lap, arches his body powerfully away from her, and looks at her as though trying to see her from a new perspective. She gazes back at him smiling widely, for he is arching away from her, and it's the first time that he hasn't been simply clinging and molding. She is surprised and pleased at his strength. She lets him stand and dig and strain, until finally he relaxes and molds against her, laying his head softly on her shoulder.

As she watches, his eyes begin to droop. She softly hums a lullaby. His eyes open and meet hers, close again, open partly, and close, and then he is fast asleep, and that is the end of the story.

Baby Lifts
and Turns Head

This is a story about a young baby and it takes place in a lovely baby's room, a nursery, bright and clean and airy. In it there is a crib with an amusing mobile strung above it, turning colorfully as the air stirs. There's a rocker, and there mother sits. She seems vaguely familiar to you. There is a diapering table with a bath under it, and on the floor there is a soft quilt. On the quilt a little baby is lying with her face turned to one side, and she is making kicking motions against the quilt as she lies on her tummy, and her little arms are making swimming movements. Her mommy is watching her, lovingly smiling.

Just then baby lifts her head up, and mother's face shows astonishment, as baby deliberately turns her head and lets it plop down on the other side. Oh, mother is ecstatic! She rushes to the door and she calls, "Daddy, daddy, come right away. You'll never believe what she has just done." He comes down the hall, and she says, "Hurry, hurry, look, look."

He goes over to the blanket and he says, "Well, I don't see anything. She's just lying there on her quilt kicking her feet and beating her fists."

Mommy says, "But she just lifted up her head and turned it all the way to the other side."

Daddy exclaims, "No!"

And mommy says, "Yes, she did, she did! Maybe she'll do it again." As they both stand talking, baby does it again. And mommy grabs daddy's hand and squeezes it, "You see, you see! Isn't she wonderful?"

And daddy says, "She is a remarkable child. Is she supposed to be doing that already?"

And mommy says, "I really don't know, but I'm sure she's ahead of herself, I'm sure she is, she is so smart."

He exclaims, "Well of course, it stands to reason, now doesn't it?" And he puffs out his chest as he grins at her.

She looks back and says, "Oh you." When he goes back to work, mommy stands and watches her baby. Then she sits down beside her, there on the quilt, and baby tries to struggle as mommy picks her up, holds her up against her shoulder, and pats her gently. Baby clings and molds her body to her mommy, and holds her head up. Although she wavers a little, she is distinctly holding her own head up. Mommy puts her cheek against baby's cheek and murmurs little nonsense syllables into baby's ear. Baby kicks her feet, and pushes with her hands, and nuzzles and nuzzles, and then definitely makes rooting movements like the little piggy that she is.

Mommy says, "OK, OK, I know it's feeding time, and you shall have what you want." She takes out her breast and holding baby securely in her arms, looks into her eyes, as baby seeks and finds the nipple and sucks lustily. Mommy croons a little tune, and they are making eye contact the whole time baby is nursing. Mommy is looking tenderly into her daughter's eyes, and her daughter is staring dreamily into her mommy's face. Still looking into her mommy's eyes, she keeps on sucking until she has finished nursing.

Then mommy puts her back down on the quilt, tummy down, with her face turned to the side, and rubs her back gently, patting her behind until a big air bubble comes out, and mommy says, "That's fine, that's wonderful." Baby starts practicing turning her head. Mommy laughs, then turns baby over on her back, and baby beats the quilt with her heels, and beats the quilt with her fists, and mommy puts a rattle near her hand.

Baby grasps the rattle tightly but when it makes a noise, she looks at it with astonishment, as if to say, "What is that?" It is apparent that she doesn't understand that it is her hand moving the rattle that makes the noise, but she is intrigued. She looks at it, and then looks back into mommy's eyes, and mommy smiles at her. Then the rattle makes another noise, and again baby is startled and this time she drops the rattle. Mommy picks it up and puts it back in baby's hand. She immediately grasps it, and again it makes a noise. This game goes on until at last she drops the rattle and her attention seems to fade.

Mommy picks her up, takes her over to the diapering table and takes off her diaper, but just as she puts a clean diaper under her, baby starts to wet again. Mommy looks at her. Baby is thoroughly enjoying herself, kicking her feet and waving her hands, as mommy looks at her, and she looks at mommy, and mommy laughs.

Baby makes an unintelligible sound, something that sounds a little bit like, "Loodoo."

Mommy smiles and says, "Googoogoogoo" back.

They both look at each other with love. Mommy changes her diaper again, and after wrapping her securely in her little wrapper, takes her back to the rocker. There, rocking gently, she sings a little lullaby, and baby's eyes grow heavy. Her eyelids lift again, and she looks dreamily into mommy's face, and then her eyes close and stay closed. Mommy takes her to her crib, lays her down, covers her with a soft blanket, flips on the intercom, and tiptoes out of the room, closing the door gently.

And that is the end of the episode.

Daddy Diapers Baby

This story is about a young baby. It starts in a beautiful baby's room, light, airy, and clean. In the room there is a rocker, and mommy is sitting there. In her lap is a fine sturdy baby who appears to be five or six months old. He is sitting up in his mommy's lap.

Daddy is standing beside the rocker looking down at mother and son. And daddy is saying, "My goodness, he sits so steadily now. Would you look at that." And mommy smiles proudly. She makes eye contact with her baby, who looks straight into her eyes and smiles back with complete recognition. And daddy says, "Would you look at that. Isn't that something?" Whereupon baby's eyes lift up to daddy's, and he makes eye contact with daddy. He smiles broadly, revealing two little emerging pearl-like teeth in the lower gum of his mouth. And daddy says, "Would you look at those teeth. Would you look at the size of those teeth!"

Mommy chuckles, "Oh, he is a fine sturdy fellow." The little fellow smiles again, waving his hands, and kicking his feet excitedly. Daddy lifts him up and holds him high in the air, and then brings him down and hugs him.

Mommy stands up and says, "Well, while you have him, how about going over to the diapering table now, to change those pants before lunch time." Daddy takes him over to the table and lays him down on his back. Baby squirms and kicks and goos and gurgles, and beats his little fists. Daddy takes off his diaper and wipes him. He puts the diaper in the pail, and takes out another one.

Mother sees that the baby's penis is standing up, and she yells,

"Watch out!" But it is too late. A sturdy stream of pee arches up, and hits daddy right on the chin.

Daddy grabs a diaper, wipes his chin, and says, "You little devil, you." Then he laughs, and mommy laughs, and baby smiles more proudly than ever, enjoying his exploit, and gurgling in imitation of the laughter. Then daddy gets another diaper and says, "Now, you little devil, you be careful where you aim," and he proudly diapers his son.

Then mommy reaches out and takes her big sturdy boy. She holds him half sitting, half reclining in her lap, and takes out her breast. Baby sucks noisily and enthusiastically, but soon stops. Mommy holds him upright and pats him vigorously on the back. He burps lustily and mommy says, "That's my fine boy."

Daddy gets the high chair, picks up his little son and puts him in the chair. Mommy says, "I'll be right back, right back. Here is some water, and I'll be right back with lunch." She hurries out.

Baby looks after her. His eyes stay focused on the door, and his little face goes blank. He seems, almost, to go into a trance. He becomes immobile and passive. And even though daddy tries to distract him, and to play, baby still sits there passively looking at the door. When mommy reappears, his eyes light up, and he comes back to life.

He picks up the spoon on the tray of his high chair, and bangs loudly, kicking his feet, and gurgling and cooing. Mommy exclaims, "What a greeting, what a greeting," as she sits down in front of the high chair holding his little hot dish in front of her. She dips her spoon into the pureed peas, and scoops a little up on it. Baby's mouth opens at the sight. She puts the spoon partly in baby's mouth, and tips it up so the mashed peas adhere to the roof of his mouth. Baby starts smacking and sucking, and sucking and smacking, and then swallows. Mommy repeats this maneuver, and pretty soon the peas are gone, half down baby's throat, and half smeared on his face and front.

Then mommy starts feeding him the mashed bananas. This is a favorite food, and he kicks his heels, waves his hands, and smiles. Then he looks impatient. He is about to start to cry. She makes haste to feed him the bananas, and daddy says, "What an appetite! What a buster! Good night! What a buster!" Daddy is popping his buttons with pride. And so the feeding continues, half down the front of the bib, and half inside baby. Mommy is having a great time, and so is daddy. All three are having a great time.

[59]

When lunch is finished, mommy takes her son over to the diapering table, washes his face, and takes off the spattered bib. Then daddy says, "Well, I'm going to leave you two, now. I have just a little more to finish before we have lunch, dear." He leaves, and mommy continues taking care of their baby.

She takes him back to the rocker. She holds him tenderly. He snuggles up to her, although twice he wiggles free, leaning back to make eye contact with her, and to smile again.

Now he's getting sleepy, so she begins to rock gently and to sing a little lullaby. He gradually relaxes out of his sitting position, and rests back in her arms. His eyelids grow heavier and heavier, as she sings a little song: "Loo loo loo loo bye bye, up in mommy's arms be creepin', and soon you'll be asleepin', singing loo loo loo loo. . . . " Baby's eyes close completely, and his sturdy body has grown limp in her arms. She quietly gets up, carrying her heavy little son over to his crib. There she lays him, on his belly, with his head turned to one side. She covers him tenderly, turns on the intercom, and tiptoes out of the nursery.

He has a wonderful sleep, and when he stirs again, mommy is instantly there by the side of his crib. She sees that he has turned himself over and is now lying on his back. He has kicked the covers off, and he is beating on the side of the crib with his rattle, looking at it with surprise at each jingle, looking at his hands and then beating again.

His eyes shift to the mobile. They follow the colored discs as they drift around in the shifting air. He is enjoying life completely.

Then he turns his head to his waiting mama. Their eyes meet and they both smile. He holds his hands out, still hanging on to the rattle, and she gently picks him up. She has given him time to wake completely, not hurrying him, giving him time to get his bearings, to see and hear and feel where he is . . . from out of limbo to back into here. She knows he needs time.

Now that he is looking into her eyes, and smiling at her, she picks him up, and carries him to the diapering table. And this time as she tends him, she says, "Oh my, you be careful where you aim now. No tricks." And she laughs out loud. He smiles back at her.

And that is the end of this story.

Separation and Individuation

Mommy Disappears

The next episode begins when baby has turned over in her crib. Her mommy is standing by the crib looking down. Baby looks up at her and smiles. Mommy smiles too and says, "Hello, sweetheart. Are you waking up?" Baby kicks her feet and hits her fists against the mattress ecstatically. Then she reaches for her rattle and bangs it against the bars of the crib, looking at mommy, and laughing. Mommy picks her up and sets her down in a sitting position on the blanket on the floor. There baby sits with her legs spread wide and her hands waving in front of her, laughing and looking at mommy.

Mommy says, "I'll bet my baby's hungry for lunch." Baby smiles and laughs and beats the palms of her hands on the blanket. Mommy goes to the corner to fetch the high chair. She picks baby up and straps her securely in it.

"I'll be right back with lunch, darling. Mommy will be back in a second." She hurries out the door, leaving it ajar. Baby's smile fades off her face as she looks at the doorway, the empty doorway where mommy has disappeared. From the stunned expression on her face, she seems to be saying, "Mommy has vanished forever." She keeps looking at the empty doorway, quiet, expressionless, and fixed, almost as though in a trance, withdrawn. And then mommy comes back in the room, and baby's eyes light up.

She opens her mouth and starts to wail. Mommy hurries over, puts the plate down on the tray, unfastens the strap, and picks baby up out of the high chair. Holding her close, she rocks back and forth, standing there by the chair. Then she sways from side to side and croons, "There, there, darling, mommy's here. Mommy's here. There, there, darling, mommy's here. I told you I'd be gone for just a minute and

[63]

here I am." Baby's sobs subside and smiling tearfully, with her cheeks wet, she buries her head in her mommy's neck and puts her arms around her mommy tightly.

After a few moments mommy sits her down in the high chair again. She puts mashed peas on the end of a tiny spoon. Baby opens her mouth like a little bird, and mommy manages to pop the peas into her mouth before baby has a chance to spill them off. Baby looks surprised, and smiles with her mouth full of peas. Then she starts to mash them between her gums and to swallow. With the next spoonful baby reaches out and grabs the spoon, and guides mommy's hand holding the spoon into her mouth. And mommy says, "That's fine, darling, that's wonderful." But with the next spoonful baby grabs mommy's hand and turns the spoon upside down. The peas dribble down onto her bib. She looks down at her bib in astonishment, and mommy laughs, "We have to keep the spoon right side up, don't we?"

Then mommy picks up a cup. This is somewhat more difficult. The cup has a spout, a little flat spout. She holds it up to baby's mouth and baby starts to suck on the spout. Mommy laughs and says, "Not a nipple, darling. I'll tip it and you will see." She tips it a little. Baby keeps on sucking but she gets a mouthful and chokes. She looks at mommy with big eyes, and mommy says, "We'll have to take it slower, won't we, darling?"

And so they practice, and after a while mommy praises her, takes off the spattered bib, wipes her small face all smeared with peas, and then holds her to her breast. Baby finishes her lunch, nursing.

Soon she is asleep again, and this time mommy puts her down on her tummy on a blanket on the floor.

And after a brief nap, baby is up and feeling playful. So mommy sits down on the blanket beside her. Baby sits up and then twists around and plops down and starts to reach for a little teddy bear sitting on the edge of the blanket. When she grabs it with both hands, she completely loses her balance. She and teddy go down, kerplop, on the blanket. She looks back at mommy with alarm, and mommy says, "Whoops, that didn't work." Baby echoes mommy's smile, turns around and sits up with teddy. Then she proceeds to bang teddy up and down, up and down on the blanket between her legs.

And that is the end of the episode.

Before Separation

This story is about a baby who is smiling and laughing and responding, not with words, but clearly reacting vigorously to her world. She looks familiar to you. She is in her own room, her nursery, a bright, inviting room. She is sitting on a quilt in the middle of the floor playing with her teddy bear, shaking it, biting it, putting it down, picking it up, knocking it over, and laughing. Mommy is sitting in the rocker watching the fun.

Daddy comes into the room. Baby looks up and gives him a big smile. Daddy smiles back and holds out his arms. Baby holds out her own chubby arms as daddy reaches down, lifts her and holds her high in the air, saying, "Weeeeeeeee, baby can fly, baby can fly." Baby laughs ecstatically. Then daddy brings her down to his shoulder and puts her little fat arms tight around his neck and snuggles. Then he holds her away at arms' length. Baby looks over at mommy to make sure that mommy is watching. Only then can she turn back to daddy.

Daddy says, "I'm going to sit down on your chair here and we will play a game." He sits down, and baby sits on his knees, facing him. He puts his hands up in front of his face so that his face is hidden, and baby looks at him startled. "Has daddy disappeared?" And then he parts his hands and he looks at her and says, "Peek-a-boo!" Then he closes his hands again. She laughs with delight, and he does it again. "Peek-a-boo!" She laughs again bubbling with joy. And he says, "Well, if you like it so much . . . " He takes her little hands and he claps them together in a patty-cake and he says, "Now you can applaud." She laughs. She has such fun with daddy that they play peek-a-boo for a long time. Mommy is enjoying it as much as they are.

Finally daddy puts baby down on her blanket and says, "Well, I have to go now for a little while. I'll see you later." He goes to the door, opens it, and disappears out the door. Baby sits there looking after him with big wide eyes and a solemn face because daddy has disappeared. Suddenly his face comes around the door jamb and he says, "Peek-a-boo!" She screams with laughter. Such a wonderful game, such a wonderful daddy who plays these games. She feels so good, you can see her happiness all over her eager little body.

Then mommy picks her up, holds her in her lap and puts her arms around her. How relaxed, how tender, and how loving mommy is, how patient, how calm. You can see, by the way that they look at each other, the beautiful bond between them, the trust and the telepathic understanding between them. Mommy seems to know, before baby expresses it, what it is she wants and what it is she needs. Now she looks at baby and she says, "Uh oh, I think we have full pants." Baby looks at her intently, and smiles.

So in a moment, without haste, mommy gets up and takes her over to the diapering table. She removes her diaper. Sure enough, baby has produced a fine BM. Baby looks at mommy, who exclaims, "What a fine production!" Baby laughs and mommy laughs. Mommy then proceeds to clean her, gently, without hurry, and baby seems to be aware of mother's enjoyment of caring for her. They are a very happy pair, very happy.

This little bundle of vitality and love was so recently a part of her mommy's body, and now is beginning to develop into her own person. She is her own person trying to crawl, but still looking back at mommy whenever she does, just to be sure mommy is there. And then happily trying again, but looking back each time.

And then mommy says, "Well, I think it's time to eat and so I'll be gone for just a moment, darling. Here's your teddy again, play away, and I'll be back in a second." She goes out of the room and closes the door. Baby stops laughing and sits with her little back straight and her little face blank watching the place where mommy has disappeared. Not crying, not panicked, but blank, as though part of herself has disappeared. And so she sits, not playing, not moving, just watching, until the door opens again and her mother comes in with her dinner.

Mommy smiles at her, and baby starts to smile, but then lets out a loud wail. "Ohhh," cries mother, "Goodness sakes alive, what is it, precious?" She puts the plate down, lifts baby up and holds her close, rocking her gently back and forth, patting her and crooning, "Oh my little precious, oh my sweet. Mommy is here, I'm here, darling. Did you think I disappeared? Well, I'm back, just as I said, so now let's have our delicious supper." Baby, with tears on her cheeks, gives her mommy a big wet smile. Mommy buries her face in baby's neck and gives her a tender kiss, and then sits her down in her lap to be fed.

Baby is very eager. And mommy begins their routine: the little fist around the spoon and mommy's fist wrapped around baby's fist. They dip into the mashed bananas, which is baby's favorite, and they scoop up a little. Then mommy guides the spoon to her darling's mouth. The little mouth opens like a bird's but she doesn't know how to close it to get the banana. So mommy manages to shovel it in. But half is in and half is out, and they both laugh. This goes on until mommy says to baby, "All gone." And baby's eyes get big and sparkly. She recognizes those words and laughs with delight.

And that's the end of that episode.

Separation

This is a story about a baby, a young baby who looks familiar to you. She is sitting on her mommy's lap in a nursery. It is a lovely, cheerful, bright nursery, with a crib, a playpen, toy shelves, and a rocker. On the floor a soft quilt is spread out and on it mommy is playing with her baby. She's giving her a rattle, and baby shakes it and then lets it fall, and looks at mommy and laughs, and mommy laughs at the game, too.

Then mommy gets up and sits in the rocker, picks up baby and props her up so that baby is almost sitting upright in her lap facing her. Then she clasps the two small hands, and she says, "Patty cake, patty cake, baker's man," and baby crows with delight. Mommy goes on, "Bake me a cake as fast as you can. Roll it, and roll it . . ." and then she marks a "B" on baby's palm. Baby squeals ecstatically, " . . . And put it in the oven for baby and me." Then she hugs her. Baby enjoys this game. Mommy is having a very good time, too.

Then baby grasps the front of mommy's dress, and pulls herself up. Mommy helps her stand up in her lap facing her. Then baby leans far back, away from mommy, and looks at her very intently from that distance. Mommy makes eye contact with her as baby continues to pull away to look at her. Then she begins to struggle and wiggle to get away. Mommy lets her slide down the front of her legs until she is down on the quilt on the floor. Then she turns baby over on her tummy, and baby promptly props herself up on her straight arms and surveys the room, looking back at mommy and smiling her lovely, wet smile.

Mommy is smiling back at her, and then, do you know, she begins to kick her feet, and it's apparent that she's trying to push herself forward. Mommy exclaims, "My, would you look at that! Would you ever look at that! I do believe she's actually crawling!" She runs to the door and calls "Daddy, daddy, come right away. You'll never believe this."

In a little while her husband comes into the room. He looks around saying, "Now what is our remarkable genius doing?"

And mommy replies, "Oh you! Just you watch and you'll see. Look at her." Just then baby starts pushing one foot and pushing with the other, and does manage, before she falls down on her face, to push herself forward a few inches.

Her daddy says, "That is remarkable! That is remarkable!" And with that baby turns over on her back, and coos and crows. Her daddy says, "That's my girl, that's my girl. Can you sit up?" She tries and she struggles as she raises her little feet for leverage, but she can't, so daddy gives her a hand and props her up. Then she sits there swaying slightly, unsteadily, but delighted with herself. Daddy exclaims, "That's wonderful. That's just wonderful." She holds out her arms, and daddy picks her up, holds her high in the air, and then brings her down for a bear hug. She is laughing, and cooing, and crowing the whole time. Then daddy hands her to her mommy and says, "Here, please take little miss now. I'm sorry, but I have to go back to work."

Mommy takes baby's hand as daddy leaves and says, "Bye bye, daddy, bye bye," and she waves baby's hand. Baby laughs aloud. Everything is such a wonderful new game. All of life is a wonderful, marvelous game.

Then soon she's struggling to slide down mommy's lap, and out of mommy's arms to get down on that blanket and start practicing again. Mommy watches as she practices turning over, struggling to sit up, pushing her feet, and trying out all her new great powers. A wonderful, wonderful time of experimenting, full of fun and games.

Finally, mommy scoops her up, holds her in her lap, and says, "Now then, you have had a good play time. I think it's time to eat and then take a nice nap." Mommy takes her breast out of the front of her dress and baby eagerly begins to suck. Mommy laughs and hums a little song, and says, "Goodness, goodness what a piggy, what a piggy this is." And as she cradles baby, she holds her two pink feet in her hand. Baby pushes her feet against her mommy's palm and goes on sucking eagerly.

When she's been burped, and then diapered, mommy puts her down in her little crib on her tummy. Baby reaches her arm around and, quite by accident, finds her fist. Then she finds two fingers that

[69]

she puts in her mouth and she starts sucking busily. Her eyelids close and open, and close again and open, and finally stay closed. Mommy turns on the intercom, covers her with her blanket, and tiptoes out of the room.

And that's the end of that story.

Learning to Crawl

This story is about a little boy, still quite a baby. He is sitting up in his mama's lap. She's sitting in a rocking chair in a beautiful room. It's a baby's room with shelves all along one wall, crowded with toys. The baby is making grasping movements on his mama's dress, and is trying to pull himself upright in her lap as he digs his feet down to get his balance on the top of her thighs.

His mama laughs, puts her hands up under his armpits, and holds him up. As she hugs him tight against her, he puts both little fists against her chest and pushes himself back as far as he can. He looks at his mother, distancing as far as he can get by straining away. He looks at her. She is looking back, making eye contact with him. There is a questioning ock on her face. Baby is very serious and very intent. Then he squirms and wiggles. He wants to get down. His mama smiles and lifts him down. She puts him on the blanket, and he sits there erectly, with his little back very straight, and his widespread legs giving him balance.

He waves his hands and looks around, away from mommy. Suddenly he turns, but he loses his balance and lands kerplop on his side. Mama, in a reflex action, reaches out to steady him, but then stops herself to see what he will do. He starts to cry, so she gets down on the floor beside him and pats his bottom, as she murmurs little soothing noises in her throat, "Oh, oh, oh." Baby looks back at her over his shoulder, stops crying, and raises himself up with his arms straight, pulling his chest up off the floor. With his head turned back to look at her, and with a little frog-like motion, he kicks his feet and manages to push himself forward a couple of inches.

Again he falls, and turns around to look at mommy. She is smiling at him encouragingly, saying, "Very good, very good, I think you're learning to crawl." So he decides not to cry, and does the little frog push again. Then he gets one leg higher than the other, and really pushes with that one. He actually scoots ahead to the edge of the blanket. His mama applauds, "Hooray. That's wonderful," says she, "Wonderful! I do believe you're learning to crawl."

Exhausted, he lies flat, with his head turned to one side. After resting a little, he gives a mighty heave, and rolls himself over on his back. Struggling and pushing, he manages to sit up, and mommy applauds again, "That's fine. That's fine." But he isn't paying attention. He is looking with astonishment at the rattle that has just made a noise when he pushed against it. And then, looking at the rattle, he holds out his fist and grasps it. When it makes a noise, he looks at mommy with surprise. He keeps rattling the rattle, and laughing. Mommy is laughing, too.

Daddy comes to the door, and asks, "Now what's all this ruckus I hear in here, with laughing and banging?"

"You'll never believe it, darling. Come and see what he can do." She pulls baby up so he's half standing, and then deftly she turns him over on his tummy. Whereupon, as if on cue, he starts to push his legs, and manages to advance again, like he did before.

Daddy applauds, and says, "Hooray. Isn't that wonderful! That's great! I do believe our little Buster is beginning to crawl."

And mommy says, "Yes, he is, and he doesn't want to sit on my lap. He wants to get down, and practice."

"Well," daddy says, "I think that's great."

"It is great! I think it's wonderful." Together they beam at their little baby. Then mommy gets up off the floor. Daddy puts his arm around her shoulders and she puts her arm around his waist, and they stand watching their baby's first efforts at crawling.

As he tries to crawl, he fixes his gaze, not on his mommy, and not on his daddy, but intently on a small woolly dog that is just there beyond the blanket. Making valiant efforts to advance, pushing and pushing, at last he grasps the dog. Then he turns over on his back, waves his feet in the air, and holding the little dog in both fists, right above his face, he coos and smiles.

And that is the end of this episode.

Crawling and Playing

This story begins in a baby's room. It's a lovely room, bright, cheerful, and full of interesting things. Mommy is sitting in an armchair, relaxed and watching baby with pleasure. Baby is crawling busily around the floor, picking up a toy, discarding it, and examining another. She crawls away from mommy as fast as she can, but looks back every once in a while, checking to be sure mommy is there and is still involved with her. She picks up a ring with a little bell attached and starts biting on it, enjoying the biting, and biting away as hard as she can, grinning at mommy, and drooling as she bites.

The door opens and daddy comes in. Baby drops the ring, bounces up and down on her bottom and reaches up with her arms. Daddy picks her up and holds her high in the air, then brings her down, and hugs her tight to his chest. He rocks her back and forth, saying, "How's my beautiful big girl today?"

Baby laughs and then she covers her face with both her hands and daddy says, "Och, you want to play peek-a-boo. OK then." And he sits down with her astride his knees, and he says, "But first we'll play horsey. So, here we go." And he chants, "Trot, trot, trot, horsey and bump, bump, bump." He joggles her up and down in a trot.

She laughs hard, and then when she's laughing so much it seems as though she can't laugh anymore, daddy stops and says, "You just rode a white horse to Banbury Cross to meet a fine lady upon a fine horse, with rings on her fingers and bells on her toes," and he rings the bell on the little ring, and "she can make music wherever she goes, just like you." Baby laughs again and then they play peek-a-boo.

Mommy watches, smiling, and finally says, "Well, how about lunch now? It's about lunch time."

[73]

And daddy says, "That sounds fine to me."

And baby says something like, "Woooo," so mommy goes to prepare lunch and daddy keeps on playing. But then baby pushes him
away, and wiggles to get down on the floor. She starts crawling busily
around, looking back at daddy every once in a while as she did with
mommy. When she reaches the crib, to his amazement, she grabs
hold of the crib leg with both hands and pulls herself up on her knees,
and daddy says, "Would you look at that, I think she's trying to stand."

Mommy comes in the room and says, "Yes, she's been doing that,
pulling herself up and then looking around not knowing exactly how
to let herself down again. When she does, she plops and then she
looks around to see if that was all right or if she ought to be crying.
And, of course, I always applaud."

And daddy says, "Here, we're applauding, both applauding, hooray, that's beautiful, that's wonderful." Baby lets go and sure enough,
plops, and then she looks around doubtfully and makes a face as if to
cry. Daddy picks her up, swoops her up, and says, "There, there, it's
all right! That didn't feel good, did it? No, that didn't feel good." She
starts to cry a little, a little weepy, but without tears. And daddy hugs
and rocks and comforts.

Then they sit down to lunch, and it's daddy who feeds her. He
makes it into a lovely game with baby turning her head away, and
turning back, and then opening her mouth, and then pushing the
food out, and they have a lot of fun. More goes out than in, but
enough goes in so that mommy is relaxed and happy about it.

Then, daddy tries to hand her to mommy because it's time for
mommy to give her a little drink out of her weaning cup, but baby
wiggles and struggles away, and holds onto daddy. So daddy says,
"OK, OK, and holds her on his lap while mommy gets the weaning
cup with its little spout. Daddy holds it up to baby's mouth, and baby
looks at him, and then turns her head away and teases him.

So he says, "Oh, now we're gonna play, are we? OK then." He
holds the spout to the baby's ear, and he says, "Maybe we want to
drink with our ear this time." Baby shakes her head. Then he holds it
up to the back of baby's neck. "Maybe baby wants to drink from back
here?" And baby giggles and pushes daddy. Then he brings it around
to the front, and says, "I'll bet that there's a little mouse in the house,
right here, that's going to drink this milk right out of the spout!" And
baby's eyes widen as daddy puts the spout in her mouth and turns his
head away as he says, "I wonder if, while I'm not looking, the mouse
in the house will drink up the milk?" When he turns back again, baby

[74]

has gulped down most of the milk. He exclaims, ' Would you look at that, mommy! There is a mouse in this house, and that mouse is drinking up baby's milk! Naughty mouse!" And baby crows with joy, and claps her hands.

Pretty soon she has finished her milk and mommy says to daddy, "I think it's time now for a little nap, so would you put her down?"

And daddy says, "Yes, and if you'll swap with me, I'll sit in the rocker, because I have some songs of my own I would like to sing." And as baby snuggles up to him, he softly begins to croon a lullaby. Soon her eyes have closed and she is fast asleep. Daddy carefully lays her down in her crib and covers her gently. Together, mommy and daddy leave the room.

And that is the end of the episode.

Weaning

This story is about a baby who looks sort of familiar and so does the baby's room. Bright, clean, cheerful, there's a rocker and mommy is sitting in it. Next to the little table daddy is balancing on his haunches. They are both focusing their attention on baby.

Baby is sitting on the floor bolt upright. She is banging away with a rattle, then stuffing the end of the rattle in her mouth, then drooling and chewing and biting on it. She takes it out of her mouth and laughs with mommy and daddy about it, and then puts it back into her mouth, chewing like a little tiger cub. You almost can hear her snarling as she attacks the rattle. She snorts, and drools, and mommy and daddy are enchanted.

Then baby raises her arms toward daddy, and gives him a winning smile. Daddy is all eagerness. He leans forward and picks her up, his big hands under her little armpits. He holds her out at arms' length, and then hugs her tight. He snuggles his face in her neck, and blows "Pflooooo." She laughs a big belly laugh . . . such a funny daddy.

Then daddy sits down on the chair and puts her down astride his knees. He bounces his knees and baby bounces and has a wonderful time. Mommy is just as intrigued as baby. But baby has not once looked at mommy. Her eyes, her round wide eyes, are fastened adoringly on daddy's face.

Then daddy says, "I'm ready for lunch, how about you?"

Mommy says, "I'll get it. It's coming right up, coming right up." She leaves the room.

Baby doesn't turn and follow her with her eyes. She's completely engrossed with daddy. And so they play. They play horsy, and they play peek-a-boo, and then they start to patty-cake. Daddy holds her hands and slaps them together, "Patty-cake, patty-cake baker's man. Bake me a cake as fast as you can. Roll it . . . ," and he rolls her little hands. " . . . And roll it, and mark it with a 'B' . . ." and he marks a "B" on the palm of her hand. She giggles and wiggles because it tickles, " . . . And bake it in the oven for baby and me."

Now mommy is back with lunch. She puts it down on the tray of the high chair. Daddy lifts baby up and puts her in the high chair. Mommy takes a spoonful of applesauce and offers it, but baby turns her head away and clenches her lips together. Then she takes the spoon away from mommy and holds it out to daddy. Daddy says, "Oh ho ho, I see! It's like that, is it?"

And mommy says, "Well, all right for you!"

So daddy puts his big hand around her little fist and baby opens her mouth wide and he pops the applesauce in. Some of it dribbles down her chin, and some of it goes in, and some of it she mischievously pushes out of her mouth again, as she giggles at daddy. Daddy growls. "Oh ho, we're going to play games are we, missy? Well, now, we'll see about that." And so he starts to play. He says, "Here is a nice spoon of applesauce. Oh no, it isn't. Somebody ate the applesauce. No applesauce for baby. What is this mommy?"

And baby is watching, leaning forward, looking from mommy to daddy and daddy to mommy. Her little mouth is open and dribbling, and daddy says, "Now we pop it in." And he does when she doesn't expect it. She closes her mouth in surprise and swallows, and then grins at daddy. So they manage to get the applesauce down. Just before it's all gone, baby reaches for her weaning cup, a little cup with a cover on it and a little spout, a little flat spout. Daddy holds it up to her mouth and tilts it a little. The milk comes out of the spout into her mouth and surprises her. She chokes and sputters, and daddy says, "Oh, apologies, darling, apologies. That was too much." She looks at him with big tears in her eyes. "Oh," he says, "A naughty daddy, that's a naughty daddy. Here mommy, maybe you'd better handle this operation."

Mommy takes the cup and holds it up. Baby promptly begins to bite on the spout and mommy says, "Well, OK, get used to it. I know this is a shocker." Baby looks at her and pushes the cup away. There are tears in her eyes and she starts to wail. Mommy says, "Well, I know what you want, darling, but it is time now for you to begin drinking from a cup. You know, you've done it with your juice, and you've even done it with water. Now let's do it with milk." And so baby takes a little but then turns her head away and won't take anymore. Her mommy says, "Well, OK, maybe later, maybe later." And she puts the cup down. Baby reaches over and promptly knocks the cup off the high chair.

Daddy exclaims, "Would you look at that, now! How do you like that for spirit?" Baby looks down at the cup on the floor and then back at mommy, clearly expecting mommy to pick it up. So mommy picks it up and puts it back on the high chair tray and baby promptly knocks it off again. And again she looks at mommy expectantly. This has turned into a great game.

So mommy picks up the cup, takes baby out of the high chair and holds her in the crook of her arm. She snuggles her and then holds the spout gently up to baby's mouth. Baby is resting her cheek against mommy's breast and now she does drink a little more milk, and mommy says, "That's wonderful, darling." Baby's eyes begin to close, and mommy says, "I think our little darling is ready for her nap."

And that is the end of the episode.

Exploring Mommy

We see a beautiful room. It is a baby's room. There is a crib, and a playpen. There are shelves of toys and books, a baby's room that speaks of love. There is mother sitting in a rocker. She looks somewhat familiar to you, but you are not sure, and there is a baby who seems to be about six or seven months old. She is sitting in her mommy's lap. Mommy is smiling at her and baby is cooing and smiling back.

Baby is very busy exploring. She reaches for mommy's glasses. Mommy puts her hand up quickly to protect them, but baby tugs away and succeeds in pulling them off. Mommy chuckles and warns, "Be careful, darling, don't break them," and baby puts them in her mouth. Mommy gently extracts them, and holds up a keyring. When she jingles the keys, baby lets go of the eyeglasses and reaches for the keyring. She gurgles in triumph when she captures them. Then she looks at mommy and drops them on the floor. Mommy laughs and reaches down to retrieve them. Baby grabs them again and shakes them vigorously up and down before throwing them on the floor again. Mommy laughs, "Oh, so it's going to be a game, is it?" Baby makes gurgling noises.

Then, forgetting the keys, she starts exploring. She grabs mommy's necklace and looks at it, and then looks at mommy to see if that's all right. Mommy smiles, takes off the necklace and puts it around baby's neck. Baby is delighted and looks down at herself as she bounces in mommy's lap. Then her attention shifts to a brooch on mommy's dress. While her baby is intrigued with the brooch, mommy gently takes the necklace from around baby's neck and stuffs it in her pocket. Baby tries to pull the brooch, but it won't come off.

So she snuggles closer to mommy and starts twisting and manipulating the pin. Mommy looks at her, hugs her, snuggles with her, laughs, and distracts her.

Soon baby tires of exploring and begins to wiggle. She wants to get down off of mommy's lap and venture out into the room. Mommy says, "Oh, so we want to get down, do we?" And she helps baby slide down the front of her legs and sit on the floor. Baby sits still for a moment, then she reaches for the keys and rattles them. She is careful to stay very near mommy's feet. She looks at mommy. Mommy smiles, so she crawls a couple of feet further away, then looks back, checking to see if mommy is still watching.

When she has assured herself that mommy is indeed there, she reaches for a little toy dog that is sitting on the blanket with her. She has a good time, and mommy enjoys watching her.

Then mommy gets down and sits on the blanket with her. Baby climbs on mommy's lap and peers into her face intently. Then she puts her fingers in mommy's mouth. Mommy pretends to growl and to bite, and baby squeals with joy. They play that game for a little while, and then baby reaches up and gets a firm grip on mommy's nose. And mommy cries, "Hey there, that doesn't feel so good!" Baby laughs out loud, so mommy can't help laughing, too. Then she lifts one little finger after another off her nose as she distracts baby's attention by jingling a bracelet on her arm. But baby is too busy exploring mommy to be distracted. She reaches over and pats mommy's breast. Mommy smiles at her, so she reaches up and clutches the side of mommy's neck. And then, without warning, she reaches up and tugs powerfully at mommy's hair. Mommy squeals, "Hey, that hurts! Let go!" Baby is so delighted she bounces up and down, laughing and crowing.

Then mommy announces, "Do you know, I think it's time for lunch. Let's see." Baby sits still looking at mommy with big eyes. And mommy says, "Come on, darling, let's go get our lunch." She picks up baby and carries her like a little sack of potatoes into the kitchen, sits her down on the floor, and begins to prepare her lunch.

Baby crawls after mother, staying close to her feet. Mother warns, "Be careful, now, there's heavy traffic here. Be careful not to get trampled!" Baby bounces and coos and laughs.

Mommy picks her up and sits her in her high chair. She lowers the tray in front of her and puts baby's warming dish on it. She pulls up a kitchen chair and sits close, facing baby and says, "Now, let's eat lunch." Baby opens her mouth like a little bird. Mommy gets a bit of mashed carrots on the tip of a spoon and quickly pops it into baby's mouth. Baby looks at mommy with surprise, swallows before she realizes what has happened and then reaches for the spoon herself. Mommy lets her have it. She scoops it into the mashed carrots, comes up with a blob, and then thrusts the spoon at mommy's mouth, trying to feed mommy. Mommy laughs, and then makes a great show of smacking her lips and saying, "Yum, yum, that's very good." Then she guides the spoon back into baby's mouth. They continue this game. A lot of mashed carrots get spilled on baby's bib, and some of it on the front of mommy's apron, but they manage to have a wonderful lunch.

When finally they finish, mommy spreads her arms wide and says, "All gone!" And baby stretches her hands out wide, too. This is something she recognizes. She coos, and mommy says, "That's right, darling. That's wonderful . . . well, we've finished lunch, and now it's naptime." Baby raises her arms, and mommy picks her up out of the high chair and carries her into the nursery.

There she changes baby's diaper, and carefully wipes her face and hands. Then she sits down in the rocking chair, and cuddles her baby. Gently rocking, she begins to softly hum a lullaby. Baby pats her mommy's breast, then pats her shoulder, snuggles her face against mommy's skin, and presses her little body closer. Her eyes grow heavy and soon she is sweetly sleeping. Mommy gets up slowly, and quietly carries her to her crib. She puts her down gently and covers her tenderly. She turns, flips on the intercom, and leaves the room, closing the door behind her.

When baby wakes, mommy is there at the side of the crib. And when baby first opens her eyes, she looks up at her mommy. They both smile.

And that is the end of this episode.

Standing Up

This is a story about a young baby. The baby looks familiar to you, there in the nursery, with mommy sitting in her rocker. Baby is doing something fascinating. Mommy is watching intently, with great enjoyment. Baby is pulling herself up, hand over hand, on one of the legs of her crib, standing upright, holding on shakily, with her little bottom trembling and sticking out at an angle. She turns around and looks at mommy with joy and triumph.

Then letting go, she wavers wildly for a moment, and kerplop, bang, she sits down on her little fat bottom. Her face screws up to cry, but she looks over at mommy to see if it's all right. And mommy says, "Oh, that hurt, didn't it, darling?" Baby starts to wail, pitifully, being a little baby again. Mommy reaches down, picks her up gently, and holds her tenderly in her lap. With baby's head cradled against her breast, she rocks her and says, "There, there, my sweet, you're going to be fine. It isn't going to hurt much longer, and you are wonderful to be standing up like that. That is wonderful!" Baby stops wailing pitifully, looks up at mommy with big tears in her eyes, and snuggles up closer while mommy soothes her and rocks her like an infant again.

But soon she has enough of this, and begins to struggle and wiggle. She wants to get down. So she stands up in mommy's lap and digs her little feet into mommy's thigh. She leans back so as to get a better look at her, and then struggles harder to be let down. As soon as she is on the floor, she's off again, crawling back to the crib leg, back to her practicing, not looking at mommy at all now, intent on being on her own.

Mommy gets up and goes to the door to call daddy. "Come quick. This is something you must not miss. And bring the camera, dear."

Daddy comes dashing in, just in time to see baby standing upright with her little behind stuck out. He looks at mommy, and she looks at him. They put their arms around each other. Both have wide grins of delight when baby turns around and sees daddy. She lets go of the leg, goes bang on her fat bottom again, turns around and starts to cry.

Daddy applauds, "That was wonderful, honey. That was wonderful." He continues applauding and baby stops crying. She looks at daddy and starts to smile tearfully. She is half smiling half crying. Daddy leans over, picks her up, gives her a bear hug, puts her down and says, "Now, crawl over to that leg and do it again. That's my big girl." So she crawls over, but this time she holds on, and doesn't let go of the leg quite so soon. Daddy walks over and holds out his hands. Baby lets go of the leg and quickly puts her little hands into his, just before she collapses back down again. Daddy steadies her. She holds herself up, holding onto daddy, and both are grinning from ear to ear. It's a wonderful moment. And baby completely forgets to look over to check out where mommy is.

And that is the end of this episode.

First Step

This is a story about a young baby who looks very familiar to you. The baby is standing up on mommy's thighs as mommy sits in the rocker, and mommy is holding baby's hands. Baby is stiffening her body, and digging her little feet into mommy's thighs . . . and almost standing alone. Then baby gets down on her knees, wiggles and squirms off of mommy's lap and stands on her own two feet on the floor balancing herself with two hands on mommy's knees. She lets go of one hand, and turns her body away from mommy. To mommy's amazement and delight she takes a step away. Then she looks back at mommy with surprise. Mommy smiles and says, "That's wonderful, honey," whereupon baby sways like a little tight-rope walker, and falls down, kerplunk, on her bottom. She lets out a wail of anguish. Mommy picks her up, holds her close, and standing there, rocks her back and forth, soothing her: "There, there, there, that was wonderful! You took a step! You did take a whole step by yourself."

Then, still holding baby, she goes to the door and calls down the hall. "Daddy, daddy you won't believe this, guess who just took her first step! Come right away!"

Daddy is there almost instantly, eager to join in. Mommy takes baby back to the rocker, sits there holding her in her arms and petting her.

Baby is looking at daddy with big eyes. The tears are still brimming, and daddy says, "Oh did you fall, darling?" Baby looks at him, starts to whimper a little, and mommy pats her.

But soon baby is squirming and wiggling down off mommy's lap again and standing on her own two feet holding onto mommy's knees. Mommy says to daddy, "Did you see that?"

"I most certainly did." He applauds loudly, "Bravo! Bravo!" whereupon baby again turns, lets go of one knee, and takes a full step.
Daddy exclaims, "I'll be. Did you see that, Mommy?"

And mommy laughs, "I certainly did." Baby takes one more tight-
rope step, swaying wildly.

Daddy comes up and catches her under the arms. Then he takes
her two hands. And with daddy kneeling in front of her, she starts to
take a step. He moves one knee back. She takes another step forward.
He puts the other knee back; she puts the other foot forward. And do
you know, soon she has taken four steps and arrives at the leg of her
crib. There she hangs onto the leg of her crib for dear life.

And here is the next episode. Mommy is on her knees, and baby is
hanging onto her crib. Mommy is holding her arms out to baby so
that her hands are about two small steps away as she says, "Come on
darling, you can make it." Baby lifts one bent knee high, and takes a
staggering step. Then quickly she takes another. She starts to fall
forward but mommy catches her and holds her up. Baby crows with
delight, and mommy says, "That was wonderful."

She calls daddy again, and daddy comes. He takes one of baby's
hands and mommy takes the other. Now baby starts a little drunken
sailor walk between them. They keep pace as she walks half a step
ahead of them. They hold her hands tightly. Baby is delighted, and
mommy and daddy look at each other glowing with pleasure.

And that is the end of this story.

Walking

This story is about a little girl child. Her mommy and daddy are there with her in a lovely child's room with a crib, a rocker, an easy chair, and a playpen. There are shelves of toys on the walls. The room is bright and cheerful, colorful and clean. This is, obviously, a very lucky baby.

She is pulling herself up on her crib leg and then letting go and balancing herself, swaying a little, but balancing herself with her arms outstretched as though she were walking a tightrope. Daddy and mommy are watching her with great pleasure, and daddy says softly so as not to startle her, "That's wonderful, darling, very good, very good," and mommy says, "That is fine." And now mommy gets down on her knees a few paces away from baby and holds out her arms just beyond baby's reach. Baby takes a single step toward mommy before she starts to fall. Mommy grasps baby's two arms and holds her up, and baby squeals with delight, as daddy applauds.

"She can walk!" he says with real joy. Baby turns and grins at him with her little front teeth gleaming. Daddy stands up and helps mommy stand up. They each take one of baby's hands, and between them, they hold her up. She begins to put one foot in front of the other, and she is actually walking.

Daddy is very pleased, as mommy picks up the baby, hugs her, and says, "You are wonderful, darling, you are wonderful. You're not even a year old, and you are walking! You are really walking! Before we know it, you will be running all over this house. And then that will be something trying to keep up with you."

Baby looks at her and looks at daddy and she says, "Da Da," and he says, "That's right, honey, this is Da Da," and then she looks around, teasing, and looks at her mommy and says, "Da Da."

Mommy says, "Oh, you know better than that." And baby laughs gleefully. Then she looks at her mama, turns away, looks back again, and says, "Ma Ma." Mommy grabs her, hugs her, and says, "That's right." And now they start practicing. They walk down the corridor. Baby is taking her little staggering steps, her legs wide apart . . . taking these little balanced steps with evident satisfaction and pleasure.

And there the scene ends.

In the next episode baby is walking. She's still a little unsteady, but she's walking without holding on, ahead of mommy. She keeps looking back, and then trying to run away, and mommy is following slowly after her. Baby keeps checking to be sure mommy is chasing her, and clearly it's a game in which she is running away from mommy.

Then mommy says, "All right now, all right now, it's time to turn around and come back, time for our bath and then for our lunch. So let's turn around." But baby runs away faster, looking back over her shoulder to be sure mommy is following. Mommy just stands there. Then baby stops uncertainly, not knowing whether to run faster, or exactly what it is she wants to do. So mommy comes, scoops her up in her arms, hugs her, and says, "That's my darling little girl."

She takes her back to her room, undresses her, and pops her into the tub. Baby sits there playing with her bath toys. There is a little duck. When she squeezes it, it makes a funny quack-quack noise. And there is a fish. When she squeezes it, it spouts water, and she laughs, she splashes, and she has a high old time. Mommy has put on a big plastic apron, and is having as much fun as baby splashing in the bath.

Somehow or other she manages to soap the squirming little body, and to wash her gently and playfully. When mommy gets to baby's toes, she says, "This little piggy went to market, this little piggy stayed home, this little piggy had roast beef, this little piggy had none, and this little piggy cried, 'Wee wee wee wee' all the way home!" Baby squeals with delight. And then mommy repeats the game with the other rosy toes.

Then baby says, "Patty, patty," and they played patty-cake patty-cake, baker's man, and when they get to the part with "Mark it with a 'B', for baby and me," again there is a wonderful squeal of pleasure and fun.

At last mommy picks the little wiggling, squirming, kicking, joyous baby out of the tub, puts her up on the table, dries her thoroughly, gently, tenderly, rubs her little head to dry her hair, and gets her into clean diapers, a little shirt, and a little sleeveless dress.

Then mommy ties a big bib around baby's neck, as daddy comes in, and says, "May I join you for lunch?"

Mommy says, "Of course. Please do. Just stay here with our little scamp for a moment while I get the food."

Daddy sits down in front of baby who is sitting upright in her high chair, impatiently banging her spoon and fork on the tray, making quite a racket and having a great time. Daddy is laughing, too, and clapping in time with her banging.

Then mommy comes in with lunch. Baby starts shoveling the food in by herself. Sometimes the spoon is upside-down, and more goes out than in, but she is eating by herself. Mommy and daddy are eating, too.

Baby shoves aside her carrots and says, "NO."

Mommy says, "Oh, would you like some more carrots, daddy?"

And daddy says, "Why certainly. Do you think that it's OK to take baby's carrots?"

Mommy says, "Of course. She doesn't want them."

So daddy reaches over and puts his fork into the carrots. Baby grabs the fork, and laughs right up into his face. Then, using his fork, she puts the carrots into her mouth. Daddy says, "Oh, it's going to be like that, hm? You don't want them until I want them, is that it?" She laughs, and he laughs, and mommy laughs, and that is the way they finish lunch.

Then mommy says, "Daddy, I think the carrots are all gone."

Baby stretches her arms wide and says, "All gone, all gone," and mommy and daddy laugh, and they say, "Yes, lunch is all gone."

Mommy picks her up out of her high chair, takes her over to the bath table, wipes her face clean, and takes off the spattered bib. Then holding her gently, she carries her to the rocker, and as she rocks her briefly, she sings a little song.

Baby turns and says to daddy, "Daddy, read," and daddy says, "OK." He goes to the bookcase and gets a book, and he brings it over, puts her in his lap, and starts to read the story of *The Three Little Pigs*. When he gets to the place where the wolf is huffing and puffing, he reads, "I won't let you in, I won't let you in, not by the hairs on my chinny-chin-chin!"

Baby looks at him with big eyes, and she says, "Chinny-chin-chin!"

Daddy says, "That's right, darling," and he continues, "Then the wolf huffs and he puffs . . . "

[90]

Baby is still looking at daddy. She says, " . . . huffs and puffs!"

He says, "That's right, darling," and he goes on, " . . . but he can't blow the house in!"

Baby murmurs, "Can't blow . . . "

" . . . and the three little pigs laughed and laughed. . . . " Daddy looks down and sees that baby is fast asleep in his lap. Gently, quietly he puts the book aside, and carries her to her crib. He tucks her in, and leaves the room.

And that is the end of the story.

Toddler

The next episode takes place about three weeks after baby has learned to walk. Mommy is holding baby's hand and baby is walking, lurching rather, beside mommy. She squirms and twists her hand out of mommy's grasp and before mommy can say a word, baby is off down the hall on her own. Mommy is following behind, while baby clearly indicates, looking back over her shoulder, that she wants mommy to chase her, even though, at the same time, she also wants to run away. So mommy shuffles her feet in quick little noisy steps behind her, stamping to show that she's running and chasing. Baby crows with delight, and quickens her walking. Now mommy comes and swoops her up in her arms, holding her tight. Both of them laugh joyfully. Soon this becomes the game of the day, with baby breaking loose from mommy, running away, each time running further, with mommy chasing behind, and catching her just as she gets too far away. Both baby and mommy have a wonderful time.

And that is the end of the episode.

You and Me

This story is about a little girl who seems to be 18 or 19 months old. She is a charming and happy little girl. Just now she is busy playing in her room. It is a lovely little girl's room. Everywhere there is evidence of how treasured she is. There are shelves of toys and books, everything that any little girl could possibly want to fill her days with interest and fun.

Her mommy is sitting in a rocking chair watching her as she plays, enjoying her daughter's exuberance. The little girl is toddling around her room, fairly steady on her feet now, and very busy bringing things to her mommy and piling them up on her mommy's lap. She looks up at mommy, inviting her to play with her, and to play with the toys she's bringing her. First she brings a teddy bear. Mommy hugs the teddy bear, and then she hugs her little daughter. Then she pretends that the teddy is kissing her daughter, who kisses the teddy back. She kisses her daughter and her daughter kisses her. And they have a high old time cuddling with the teddy bear.

Then the little girl runs to the shelves and comes back with a book. She opens the book and points to a page and says, "Doggy."

And her mommy praises, "Very good! That's right, lovey. That's a doggy. And what is this?"

And her little girl answers, "Pussy-cat!"

And mommy says, "That's right, darling! What a smart little girl you are!" They keep on playing this game, turning the pages and naming the animals.

Then mommy asks, "What color is this?"

The little girl looks at her with round eyes, and a big question mark in her expression.

[93]

Mommy says, "That's red, darling. Red."

And her daughter repeats, "Wed."

"Yes, that's right!" applauds mother, and they have a very good time with the book until the little girl's interest begins to stray, and she runs away from mommy, looking back at her to make sure she is still there.

She gets her ball which she brings back to mommy and puts in her lap. Mommy balances the teddy and the book in her lap, and now holds the ball in her hand and asks, "Oh, do you want to play ball, now?"

The little girl nods her head vigorously, and mommy rolls the ball across the floor, and her daughter scrambles after it, and brings it back to mommy, who holds out her hands for it. They start a game of throwing the ball and retrieving it, throwing the ball and retrieving it. They have a great good time.

Just then daddy comes into the room. Mommy looks up and says, "Oh, hello there! Just in time to join the fun!"

His daughter runs to him and holds her arms up. He picks her up and lifts her high in the air, shouting, "Wheeeeee! Whaaaay! You can fly!" She squeals and gurgles with excitement. Then daddy lowers her and gives her a big bear hug, and sets her down on the floor. She runs, picks up her ball, and rolls it to daddy. Daddy teases, "Oh-ho, we want to play catch, do we?" And she and daddy begin a game. Daddy rolls the ball gently to her, and she rolls it back to him. He has to scramble after it, because her aim is not very accurate. They roll the ball back and forth between them. Then the little girl looks at mommy and rolls the ball to her.

Mommy says, "Oh, good! This is going to be a three-way game, I see!"

Daddy laughs. They play ball for a while. Then the little daughter's interest fades. She goes to a corner of the room and selects several large colored blocks, and she picks out another book, a stuffed zebra, and a doll. Staggering under the load of all these goodies, she manages to reach mommy. She dumps the lot into mommy's lap.

Mommy exclaims, "Oh, my goodness! Thank you! I have such a big pile of treasures in my lap that I'm having trouble looking over them to see you!" The little girl giggles, knowing that is silly.

And daddy smiles and asks, "What have you got for me?" She looks at him, puzzled, looks back at mommy and then ignores daddy. She runs to collect more toys and a big game develops to see how many things she can pile up in mommy's lap.

[94]

Soon this game begins to pall, and mommy says, "I think it's time now for your lunch and your nap. Daddy, if you two will play here for a bit longer, I'm going into the kitchen and make lunch for all of us."

"That's a great idea, mommy!" She leaves, and daddy keeps on playing with his little girl.

He says to her, "I know a game you will like!" Her eyes grow big with anticipation. "This is a game named . . . " and he hides his face behind his hands, and then he parts them suddenly, "This game is peek-a-boo!"

She giggles and holds her hands up in front of her face, parts them and squeals, "Peek! Peek!"

He shouts, "That's the idea!" And they play peek-a-boo until mommy comes in, balancing three lunches on a tray.

She puts them on a little table, and they all sit down to eat. The little girl feeds herself rather well by this time, and they finish lunch quite soon. Then mommy says, "Time to get undressed now, get cleaned up, and pop into bed for your nap, darling."

Her daughter yells, "No!"

Mommy says, "Oh yes, dear, it's time now." But her little girl struggles away from her. She does not want to be undressed. And she does not want her diaper changed. And she does not want mommy to interrupt her fun. But mommy catches her, and somehow manages to change her and get her into her pajamas. Our little girl screams, protests, and is very cross, trying her very best to delay the whole procedure. She does not like to be undressed. She does not like to be changed, and she does not like to be put to bed.

Daddy watches and comments, "My, my, what is all this ruckus about?"

Mommy explains, "She just wants to choose her own time to do these things, and I can understand that. So how about giving us a big hug, and a kiss, darling, and then POP into bed?"

Her daughter looks at her crossly and pouts, "No!"

Then daddy asks, "Well, how about a big hug for me?" But she runs to a far corner of her room, refusing to be put to bed.

Then mommy says, "Well now, let's see what is to be done about this! No hugs, no kisses! Right?" Her little girl looks at her, puzzled. And mommy says, "You don't want to hug, and you don't want to kiss. Isn't that right?" Her daughter looks at her and thinks about it, and then smiles a little through her tears, and puts her arms around her mommy's neck. Mommy says, "Oh, that feels very good! Am I

[95]

going to get a kiss?" Her little girl giggles and gives her a big wet kiss right on her cheek.

Then her daddy asks, "How about me? Do I get one?" His daughter seems to be thinking about it, and then looks at mommy and looks at daddy, and then holds out her arms to him. He shouts, "Oh, that's wonderful! I get a hug and a kiss! Now how about we tuck you in, snug as a bug in a rug, in your little bed?"

She holds on tight to him, gives him a hug and a kiss, and then, looking at him mischievously, she says, "Peek!"

"That's right! Here we go, snug in the bed, and then we play peek-a-boo. For a minute. How's that?"

She bounces up and down gleefully and says, "Peek!" So they play peek-a-boo two times, as mommy watches.

Then she says, "We'll see you in a little while. Time to snuggle down and nap." The little girl is very tired, so she puts two fingers in her mouth, and turns on her side away from them, as they quietly leave the room and gently close the door.

And that is the end of this episode.

Baby Feeds Self

This is a story about a little boy who looks familiar to you. He's with his mommy and daddy. They are all sitting at the table. His little tray has been folded back over the back of the high chair, and he is pulled up to the table like a big boy. Mommy puts his plate in front of him. It has little pieces of cut-up chicken, and it has cut-up carrots, and it has a cut-up potato, and it has a piece of homemade bread beside it. Mommy and daddy have the same lunch, but theirs isn't cut up into little pieces. And Mommy is saying to her little son, "All right, darling, there's your nice lunch, and you know that you can handle it, so pick up your spoon and fork."

Daddy says, "Mmmmm, this is good, mommy."

Mommy replies, "Yes it's very nice. It's a very nice lunch, very tasty."

The little boy looks at his plate. Then he takes his spoon and shoves the carrots aside, and then he picks up his fork and shoves the chicken aside, and then he starts eating the bread and potatoes with his fingers. Mommy says nothing and daddy says nothing. They watch covertly as they eat. After a while he starts playing with the carrots and with the chicken, pushing them around, separating them, and making little patterns with them. Mommy and daddy just keep on eating without saying anything. When it's near the end of lunch time, he has spilled most of the chicken and the carrots on the table all around his plate.

Mommy says, "Don't you want your chicken and carrots, honey?"

And the little boy purses his mouth firmly, tightly, and shakes his head vehemently.

"OK," says daddy, "may I have them?"

The little boy looks at daddy with big round eyes and he says, "No."

"Oh," says daddy, "You know how to say 'no,' all right, don't you?"

Mommy laughs and so does daddy, and mommy says, "It's OK, honey."

Daddy says, "That's fine, But I, yum yum, I would like those carrots."

Mommy says, "Well, I'll get you some more carrots, daddy. These have been pretty much used up sliding around the plate, and landing on the placemat, not to mention being made into designs."

So daddy says, "OK, mommy, could I have seconds, please?" Mommy gets up, and gets daddy a small helping of carrots and a small helping of chicken. Daddy eats them saying, "Oh, this is good, mommy," not putting too much emphasis on it. And when he has finished, they get up from the table, and mommy quickly clears everything away without saying anything at all.

The little boy looks at her and says, "Coo-kee!" But mommy says, "No cookies, no, there are no cookies."

And then the little boy bangs his feet and starts to cry.

Mommy says, "Now, now, what is this all about?" And he says, "Coo-kee, coo-kee."

Mommy looks at daddy and daddy looks at mommy and says, "There are no cookies, son, would you like an apple?"

But the little boy says, "No, no," and looks at mommy with tears brimming out of his eyes.

Mommy picks him up, and gives him a big hug, and a big kiss, and says, "If I peel an apple, and I make eyes and ears and nose and mouth on the apple, would you like that?" His eyes clear, and he smiles, and nods his head vigorously. So mommy gets a nice shiny apple, and a little sharp knife, and sits down in the rocker. She perches him on the edge of her knees, and while he watches wide-eyed with delight, she carefully cuts eyes, and a nose, and a smiling mouth on the side of the apple, just like in a pumpkin.

The little boy says, holding his hands to both ears, and pulling on the lobes, "Mama, mama, mama," and she says, "Oh, of course, the ears, darling. I almost forgot the ears." And so she cuts the ears and then hands the apple to him. He very happily sits himself down on the corner of his little blanket on the floor, and starts to eat the back of the apple, saving the face for last.

Daddy laughs, and mommy laughs, and he says to mommy in a low voice, "Have you noticed how well he's walking; he's really walking well."

"Oh yes, he's so much steadier."

Then daddy says in a louder voice, "I think that it would be a good idea if we went for a walk in the park."

"Well, you two go, because I have some things I must do today, and I've put aside this time for it. So how about the two of you going after his nap?"

And the little boy says, "No nap, no nap."

Mommy laughs and says, "Come here darling, and she picks him up and gives him a big hug, and then she sits him down on her lap and she starts to croon a little song holding him lightly against her. He snuggles up, for after all, he's very tired, and soon, as she croons to him, his eyes grow heavy. He snuggles closer to her and as she sings a little song, he falls fast asleep.

Then she carries him into his bedroom and gently lays him down in his crib. She loosens the laces on his shoes and slips them off quietly, covers him lightly with a soft blanket and tiptoes out of the room, with daddy tiptoeing after her.

As they get outside the room and softly close the door, daddy says, "We are getting a really fine big grown-up boy, aren't we, darling?"

She smiles delightedly at him and says, "Isn't he fine! Such a fine young boy."

And that's the end of the episode.

New Sibling

This story is about a small girl and her little sister. As the story begins, there is a young child standing at her mommy's knee and her mommy is holding a tiny newborn baby. Mommy is talking to the little girl saying, "This is your new little sister, darling. Say hello."

The little girl looks at her mommy and says, "No."

"Oh, then, don't you feel like saying hello yet?"

"No."

"Well, I can understand. You don't know your new sister as yet, so of course you can't say 'hello'. And, do you want to know something funny? She can't talk at all. All she can do is cry. She can't even laugh yet. But you can. So do you know what? Maybe you could teach her to laugh. Maybe you could teach her all the things you know, and help her, and help me. You and I will be partners! You will be my special partner! You will be my very, very special partner who will help me teach your little sister all the things she needs to do to grow up. Would you like that?"

She looks up at her mommy with shining eyes and says, "Oh yes, mommy, yes! Can I hold her?"

Mommy hesitates and then she says, "If I show you how, and you're very careful, of course, my darling."

The little girl sits down in the rocker that mommy has just left, and mommy steadies her. "Now you put your arm just like this, resting on the arm of the rocker, and you sit well back in it so that you feel very safe. Then gently I will put her in your lap, just so, and then put your hand just so on your baby sister's back. And I will stay right near so you will feel safe." And they do just that.

The little girl looks into her sister's sleeping face, then looks at her sister's tiny fists with all the fingers curled up. Then she looks at her mommy, and whispers, "Oh mommy, she is so little."

"Yes, and you are so big! But once you were little just like that. And I didn't have a helper like you then. So you just had to make do with me. But your little sister is so lucky! Lucky to have you!"

Her little daughter smiles up at her mommy happily and says, "OK, mommy, that's enough. You hold her now."

Mommy takes the baby gently, sits down in the rocker again, and her little girl stands there eagerly watching. Just then the baby awakens, opens her mouth, and lets out a loud wail, as she spreads her fingers out to make starfish. Mommy exclaims, "Oh, I do think that's a hunger cry."

The little girl asks, "Will I be able to tell a hunger cry, mommy?"

"Yes you will. You'll be able to tell the difference between a hunger cry, and a wet diaper cry, and a dirty diaper cry."

"Oh, will she go in her diapers, mommy?"

"Yes. Can you imagine such a thing?"

"I remember, but I don't do that anymore, do I mommy?"

"No you don't. You're a big girl now, and you know how to keep yourself nice and clean, making your 'peepee' and your 'big' in the right places."

"Yes, I do, I really do. And I never dirty in my pants."

"No, you don't, no, you certainly don't."

Meanwhile mommy is taking out her breast and holding baby up to the nipple. Her little girl's eyes get as big as saucers and she asks, "Is she hurting you, mommy?"

"No darling, she's nursing. This is how babies eat. Have you forgotten?"

"I never did that, mommy!"

"You have forgotten, my love, but this is how babies first learn to eat. They nurse. And mommy's milk comes out for baby just like it did for you."

"Oh, can I try, mommy, can I try to nurse too?"

"No darling, big girls don't do that anymore. This is just for babies. And if you did that, you would feel like a little baby again. But you are not a baby, you're a big girl. Do you want to stay a big girl?"

"Oh yes, mommy, but I would like to try."

"Well watch, and learn how you can do this yourself when you are a mommy, and that's the best way for you to learn, my love."

The little girl turns her back petulantly and walks a few steps away and sits on the floor. She begins to play lackadaisically with her dollies. Mommy suggests, "You could nurse your dolly."

The little girl's eyes brighten and she cries, "Oh, I can?"

"Yes." And so the little girl holds her dolly up to her nipple and pretends to be nursing too. And now there are two mommies sitting together having fun.

And that is the end of the episode.

Toilet Training

This is a story about a little boy. He's not a very big little boy, but he's pretty steady on his feet when he walks and runs. And he knows quite a lot of words and uses many of them. He's standing beside his daddy and looking up, way up, with his head tilted way back, up into his daddy's face, and he says, "Daddy, daddy, I made pee pee."

And daddy says, "Oh my, oh my, I see that you did. I see that you have made a puddle on the floor."

"Oh daddy," and the little boy looks as though he's about to cry.

But daddy says, "Never mind honey, let's go get some rags, and let's go get a little pail of water, and let's clean it up." And together they do. Then daddy helps change the little boy's clothes and clean him up nice and dry. The little boy seems very happy about it.

Then daddy says, "And now come along with me, champ, I'm going to show you something." His son confidently holds out his hand. Daddy takes it and together they walk to the bathroom. Daddy goes into the bathroom and his little son follows him. Then daddy goes over to the toilet, and he raises the seat. The little boy is looking at daddy with big eyes. Daddy stands there as he unzips his trousers, and he takes out his penis. Then he proceeds to urinate into the water in the toilet. The little boy is looking at his daddy's penis with wide eyes, and then up at his daddy's face, and his daddy sees the wonder, and perhaps . . . is it fear in his little son's face? He puts his hand on his son's head, and he says, "This is how big men do it, son. This is how to do it."

The little boy looks at him and says, "I'm not big enough."

[103]

And daddy says, "Well, that's true, you couldn't reach, standing there. But I am going to have a surprise for you this afternoon."

"Oh daddy, what, what?"

Daddy reaches over, flushes the toilet, walks over to the basin and washes his hands. His son is watching his every move, and daddy says, "I've just made a plan. You and I are going to the store."

"Oh goody, goody," the little boy exclaims, "store, car, go in the car."

And daddy says, "Yes, we're going to take the car and you're going to go for a ride with me. Would you like that?"

"Oh yes," and he jumps up and down. Daddy takes his hand and they leave the bathroom.

They go to find mommy, and daddy says, "Well, we're off about men's business."

She looks at him with surprise and asks, "Men's business?"

"Yes. We're off to find a little step stool for the toilet."

"Oh," wonders mommy, "Oh, I see. Well that's interesting."

So daddy and his little son go out and down the steps and into the car. And they start their ride to the store. The little boy is all excited, full of anticipation. This is going to be great. He's going to the store to go shopping with daddy. That is so exciting! They drive to the parking lot, and they park. Together they go into the store. His little son is half running, half skipping beside him. They go into the big store. Daddy walks over to the information desk to find out where they sell step-stools for toilets.

As they go up into that section, the little boy is busy with, "Oh, look at this, daddy, can I have it?"

And daddy says, "No, remember we've come for the step stool."

"Oh yes, oh yes!" And so they proceed with many stops along the way to examine all the wonderful things they pass. Finally they get to the step stool department and daddy finds a salesperson and they follow him to a corner of the department where there are all kinds of things. There are little step stools that have handrails. Then there are regular little toddler seats to put on the toilet seat. And then there are the little seats that are quite independent with a little pot under them that sit by themselves on the floor. The little boy is looking at all of them with wonder.

Then he looks at daddy and he says, "Toilet," and daddy says, "That's right."

Then daddy says to the salesperson, "We're looking for one that will be just right for this little boy so that he can climb the steps

[104]

himself and stand tall, and go to the toilet by himself like a big person."

"Oh yes, I have just the thing." He leads them over to a little step stool that has very shallow steps. It also has side rails, and he says, "Here you are, young fellow, try this."

Eagerly he climbs on it, and quickly reaches the top step. He stands there and looks at daddy, asking, "Is this just right, is this just right?"

And daddy says, "I think so, I think this is just right."

"Oh," the little boy cries, "Then I can do just like you do, daddy."

His daddy smiles at him happily and says, "That's right, that's right." And so they make their purchase and daddy signs the slip. He has it wrapped, and together they leave the store eager to get back home and try the step stool.

When they get home and daddy unwraps it, mommy looks at it and says, "That looks like a fine piece of equipment."

The little boy giggles, "Daddy bought, daddy bought."

"Yes, I see, daddy bought."

Her husband smiles at her and smiles at his son, and the three of them go to the bathroom.

Then daddy says, "This is men's business, mommy."

So mommy says, "Oh, excuse me," and she goes off down the hall.

Then daddy goes in and puts the little step stool down in front of the toilet. He carefully raises the toilet seat. Then he says, "Now, you climb up, son, and pull down your pants and see if you can reach."

The boy climbs the step stool, and pulls down his pants. But then he looks at daddy very uncertainly, and looks down into the toilet. His eyes are wide and he says, "I can't."

Daddy says, "Well, that's all right. We'll wait till you can."

But the little boy stands there, uncertainly, not knowing whether to climb down again or to stand there and wait.

Then daddy says, "Come with me. Pull up your pants, and we'll leave the step stool here, and when you feel you can, we'll come back."

"OK," the little boy says happily, "OK." And together they leave.

Then daddy says, "Now son, you go on into the playroom and find something to do, while daddy finishes his work. But anytime you feel you can, just come and knock on my door and I'll be there."

And that is the end of the first episode.

This is the second episode about the little boy, his daddy, and the step stool:

[105]

In about an hour, daddy hears a knock on the door. He springs to his feet, rushes out, and asks, "Now?"

And his son says, "Ready, daddy, ready."

Together they hurry down the hall. Daddy is a couple of paces ahead. Daddy wants to make it in time. His little son follows happily behind. Then, on his own initiative, he holds the handrails firmly in his two pudgy hands, and climbs up one step at a time to the top. He lets down his pants, and stands there a moment. Then he looks up at daddy, feeling a little anxious, and then looks down into the water. Daddy reaches over and turns on the tap in the washbasin, just a trickle, and to the little boy's delight he starts to urinate into the toilet.

"Look, daddy, look daddy, look what I doing, look what I doing, just like you daddy."

And daddy says, "That's right, that's right, now you are a big boy." His little son is very pleased. "Now, you wait till the end, till there is a last drop, and you can give it a little shake, and then you pull up your pants, and climb down. Next you go and wash those grubby paws."

His son protests, "I can't reach to wash, daddy."

"Of course you can't," says daddy, "so, then, let me show you something else. See if you can carry the little stepstool over there." The little boy tries to carry it, but it is too big for him. So daddy says, "The floor is very slippery. Try just pulling it like a little wagon." And his son pulls it. With joy he finds that he can easily move it over to the sink, and he can easily push it around into position, and can easily step up on it, and easily reach the water, which he does. The expression of triumph on his face is all the thanks his daddy needs.

After that, they leave the bathroom and daddy walks down the hall and says to mommy, "Guess what?"

And the little boy cries, "Let me tell, let me tell," and he says, "Mommy, I tinkle in the water in the toilet."

Mommy looks at him with wide eyes of astonishment, "You're kidding! You really did?" And he nods his head vigorously. She says, "You are very, very good to do that. That's very good for someone as little as you."

"I'm tall on the step stool, mommy."

She says, "Yes indeed, and you're tall in other ways too, my darling."

And that is the end of the episode.

Playground Fight

This is a story about a little boy who looks familiar to you, and his daddy, who also seems to be someone you know. The two, daddy and son, are walking along at the edge of a park. They are going to a playground. The little boy is skipping ahead, turning around and chattering away with his daddy. His father is smiling and responding to him. They are having a good relaxed time.

The little boy runs ahead when he sees the playground. He heads for the sandbox. Daddy follows at a leisurely pace. His son climbs into the sandbox and sits down. He looks across at another little boy who is sitting there in the sandbox filling a bucket with a small shovel. The young boy looks at him with big round eyes, looks at the shovel and looks at the bucket. Then, ignoring the bucket and several shovels that are near him, he resolutely crawls over in the sand and takes a firm grip on the other little boy's shovel. Then he grabs the bucket and tries to make off with it. Whereupon the other little boy struggles, hangs onto the shovel, yells, hollers, and starts to cry.

The little boy's mother runs over and says, "There, there, there are plenty of shovels and plenty of buckets for everybody!"

But our little boy looks at her and sticks out his underlip: "No! Mine."

His daddy comes up. "Well, now, let's see what is going on here?" Our little boy, when he sees his father, takes courage and summons extra strength. He wrests the shovel out of the other little boy's fist. Then he grabs the bucket. And to add insult to injury, he hits the other little boy on the head with the bucket.

"Oh, my!" exclaims daddy, "My my my my, what are we doing here? This won't do at all. Let me have a look." He picks up the other little boy, who is howling mightily, and examines his head. Then he turns to the little boy's mommy and says, "Well, I can see that this bump hurts, but I don't think anything serious has happened. Do you?"

She looks at him and frowns, "I hope it isn't serious," as she takes her little boy and holds him. He just screams louder and says, "I want my bucket, my shovel, my bucket."

Daddy kneels down and says to his son, "Give me the bucket and the shovel, son."

His son looks at him, sticks out his lip and says, "No! Mine, mine."

Daddy says, "Well look, I'll trade you. Here is this beautiful bucket. Look, I think it's even bigger. And here is a wonderful shovel. These can be yours. Now, you give his bucket and shovel back to the little boy."

"I won't."

"Well," says his daddy, "then I'm terribly sorry. If you can't play in the sandbox and have a good time, I guess we'll have to go home."

His little boy looks at him and two big tears form in his eyes. "Nooo," he says, "noooo. I want to stay and play."

"Well, good," says daddy, "that's what I want to do, too. So come on, let go of the bucket. Hand it over."

The other little boy's mommy tries to make it easy. She offers, "Here let me take it, honey, and I will give it back for you. I know that you just wanted to have a nice toy and you didn't notice."

"I want THIS bucket," he yells.

And daddy says, "Well, if that's how it's going to be, son, I guess we've had it for today. Maybe we'd better postpone playing here until the next time I bring you back. How is that? And we'll see if next time you can play and have a good time with the other children."

"No," yells the little boy. He turns and pushes the bucket and the shovel at the other boy and says, "There, take your old bucket, take your old shovel." Daddy looks at him and smiles a little. He looks at daddy, then he looks away, then he picks up the other bucket and the shovel, and starts filling it with sand. And after a little while he gets tired of that, and gets up brushing himself off. "Go slide, daddy."

His daddy walks over to the slide with him. The little boy climbs up the ladder and sits at the top. Daddy stands at the bottom to catch him. As he slides down, daddy goes, "Wheeeeee," and they both shout with laughter. The little boy runs back as fast as he can to climb the stairs again.

Just then along comes the other little boy and his mommy. She is smiling. Her little boy is running ahead. He climbs up the ladder just after the first little boy, who turns around, looks down at him and says, "Get off my ladder. Get off."

The little boy looks at him with big eyes and says, "It's not your ladder, it's the playground's ladder. Everybody uses the ladder."

The little boy looks at his daddy and says, "Daddy, my ladder."

But daddy replies, "I'm afraid not, son. The slide belongs to everyone, and we all take turns." His little boy looks at him, and daddy says, "Come on, let's slide down and have fun like we had before."

The little boy smiles, lets go, and "wheeeeee," down the ladder he slides. Daddy picks him up and sets him on his feet, and he runs back to climb the ladder again. Meanwhile the other little boy is sliding down, and before he knows it, he is shouting "wheeeeee" with the second little boy. Then they look at each other, and they both burst out laughing.

After this, they take turns. First our little boy, then the other little boy, then our little boy, then the other little boy, and pretty soon they're having a high old time, "wheeeeeeing" for each other.

Then they run off together and get on the seesaw. Our little boy is a little heavier than the other boy, so his side of the seesaw is down and the other little boy is high in the air.

They can't make it go, so daddy says, "Well, just a minute now, you two. Let me adjust it." They clamber off and daddy fixes it. Then they start bouncing up and down, up and down, see saw, see saw. Daddy laughs and applauds and the boy's mommy laughs and applauds, and the two little boys play together, having lots and lots of fun.

After a while, daddy says, "Well, son, I guess it's time now to start home."

"Oh, just a little bit longer, daddy, just a little longer, daddy."

Daddy says, "OK, let's see. Two more minutes, how's that?"

"OK, OK!" And they seesaw for two minutes.

Then daddy says, "OK, off we go." They steady the seesaw and both little boys climb off. Daddy says, "Say 'bye' to your new friend."

Our little boy waves and says, "Bye bye."

Daddy suggests, "Maybe tomorrow."

His little boy laughs and says, "Yes, tomorrow."

And the mommy says, "Yes, tomorrow. Have a good lunch." And off they go.

And that is the end of the episode.

[109]

Father and Son Play Catch

We see a little boy who seems familiar to you. He is standing at the door, the front door of his house, with his nose pressed against the glass watching his daddy come up the steps. The little boy is jumping up and down with happiness, and calling over his shoulder, "Mom, dad's home, mom, dad's home." Dad comes in the front door, passes his hand roughly and playfully through his son's hair, hugs him against his side, then turns and holds his arms out to his wife and kisses her.

The little boy asks, "What's in the package, dad?"

His father looks at him teasingly, and says, "Now wouldn't you like to know."

"Oh, come on, dad, come on, what's in the package? Is it for me, dad?"

His dad glances significantly at his wife, who looks at him ironically and says, "Well, is it for him or is it for me, dad?"

Dad laughs and he says, "What about for both?" He takes his hand from around in back of him and hands her a little bouquet of spring flowers.

"Oh! How lovely," as she kisses him on the cheek. "I'll go put these in water."

"What's for me, dad, what's for me?" Dad unwraps a package and holds up a baseball glove, a small baseball glove just the right size for the little boy's hand. "Oh, wow, dad," the boy says, "for me?"

And dad says, "Right on."

"Oh, wow, let me try it on." And he tries it on, holding it up. He smacks his little fist into the palm of the glove as he has seen them do at the ballpark, and he struts around trying to look very tough and very much like a pro ballplayer.

His father praises him, "Real good! You know how to do that very well. And how's this for starters?" as he tosses him a softball.

The little kid catches it, drops it, picks it up, and dad says, "That's very good, but this is also the last time we throw a ball inside the house. Agreed?"

"Sure dad, sure. So when can we go out and practice?"

Dad says, "How about right after dinner?"

"OK, OK, dad." They both go into the kitchen and he asks, "Well when's dinner, mom?"

Her son holds up his new glove. "Oh, isn't that great! What a surprise, honey. Aren't you pleased?"

And he says, "Yep, yep," hanging adoringly on his father's arm and looking up into his eyes. At last they finish dinner, somewhat awkwardly, since the boy refuses to take the glove off. He insists on eating with one hand while balancing the glove against the plate with the other.

Mother and dad are laughing at him, and mom says, "You'd get through a whole lot faster if you would put the glove down and eat your dinner, son."

But he protests, "Oh, mom, I just can't take it off." They both laugh, and finally dinner is over. The little boy urges, "Now, dad, now?"

His dad nods, "Sure enough." They get up and his dad takes his own glove out of the hall closet, puts it on, grabs the ball, and together they go out to play catch. They cross the street and head for an open stretch in the park across from their house.

Dad stands away at what he judges to be about the right distance. He tosses the softball underhand, to his little son. The ball flies far to the left, and his little son, on his short legs, doesn't get there in time. The ball bounces a couple of times away from him. He scrambles for it, picks it up, and looks at his dad questioningly, as if to say, "That was pretty punk, dad . . . was that pretty punk?"

Dad smiles and says, "We need practice, don't we son?"

The little boy perks up, grins and says, "Yeah, let's practice. PLAY BALL!" He tosses the ball underhand to his father. It falls a little short.

Dad scrambles to pick it up, just misses it, finally picks it up and says, "Hey, I'm out of practice. We really need this practice, don't we,

[111]

son?" Then he shortens the distance between them. He lobs an easy one underhand and guess what! The boy catches it. "'Ray," they both yell, "Hooray," and both grin from ear to ear.

And so the ball practice goes on. The little boy actually begins to get better at catching the ball that very first evening. We can see how proud he is, and how proud his dad is of him. Finally dad says, "Hey, now, it's beginning to get a little dark. Let's postpone this until next time."

"Hey, can we practice a lot, dad? Are you going to practice with me a lot, dad?"

"You betcha, you betcha. And after a while, when we can both catch this ball very well, I'm going to buy you a bat."

"Oh, gee, dad, that's wonderful! Oh boy, oh boy, when are you going to do that, dad?"

"Just as soon as we both get better at catch, then I'll buy you a little bat, and I'll get mine out here, and we'll practice hitting the ball."

"Oh, dad!"

And dad adds, "Yep, this is baseball summer. This summer you and I are going to be great baseball players."

The little boy runs up to him, throws his arms around his thighs and hugs him, "Oh dad, you sure are swell. You're a swell dad."

He reaches down and gives his son a long hug, saying, "Well, you're a swell son. So let's make tracks for home."

The two of them happily cross the street, go in the front door, and yell, "We're home mom," and she calls, "I'm in here, come in here."

And that is the end of the episode.

Oedipal Phase

When I Grow Up, Daddy

This is a story about a little girl. It begins in her room, a familiar room to you. It's lovely; it's bright and sunny and clean and full of happy colors. There is a small junior bed and there are toys and shelves and books, a rocking chair and a child's table with three chairs. Daddy is sitting in the rocker and the little girl is puttering around the room, happily carrying on a sort of chattering conversation with her daddy: "Oh, here is this nice dolly, daddy, did you see? Lookit, daddy, lookit, this is my new dolly." She runs and shows him.

Daddy smiles at her, strokes her hair, and says, "Oh, pretty dolly. What is her name?"

His little daughter replies, "Her name is like mine. She has my name."

"Oh," says daddy, "and what are you doing without a name?"

"Oh, DADDY," she cries, "you're teasing me! You know I still have my name! We can both have my name."

And he says, "That's true, that's true."

"Daddy, will you read me a story?"

But daddy says, "Well, I thought perhaps we would go for a walk in the park."

"Oh, goody, daddy." And she runs to get her coat. After he helps her on with her coat, she turns around and says, "How do I look, daddy?"

And her daddy replies, "You look beautiful, princess." She smiles up at him full of joy and takes his hand in both her hands and pulls and skips ahead of him down the hall and out the front door.

"Hold on, princess, waaaait a minute. Don't we want to say goodbye to mommy?" Princess looks at him impatiently, so he adds, "Well, I want to say goodbye to mommy," and he turns and leaves her for a moment. She stands there busily humming and looking out through the open door while daddy goes back to tell mommy that they're going out for a little while.

And mommy says gaily, "Have fun darling. Bye." Then she sticks her head out the door to say "Bye" to her little girl.

Her little daughter looks around and says, airily, "Bye," and they're off.

As they go down the path she says, "Look at that little girl on a tricycle, daddy. Daddy, can I have a tricycle?"

"You certainly may. I think you're big enough for a tricycle and I will teach you how to ride."

"Oh, would you, daddy? Would you? Would you, daddy?"

"Yes, darling, yes, we will get it soon. Now let me see. When is your birthday? Why I do believe you have a birthday coming up very soon."

She giggles and says, "Oh daddy, you're funny. You know when my birthday is, and it's not very soon."

"Well," says daddy, "suppose we make one up."

"Oh good, daddy, good, daddy, then I can get older faster and I can marry you sooner."

Daddy looks at her and she looks up at him, and he knows she's teasing, and she knows she's teasing. "I know, daddy, I know, daddy, you're already married, daddy, I know. And someday I'll grow up and I'll find my own prince, won't I, daddy?"

"That's right, princess, that's absolutely right."

And so they go down the path and they have a merry time. Daddy points out a little squirrel running up a tree, and then he stops and points out a flower: "These are wildflowers. We don't pick them because if we leave them, do you know what happens? They go to seed and they plant themselves and then there are hundreds more of them next year."

"Oh how nice. I won't pick them then, daddy, not even one."

They walk a little farther and daddy says, "Look what's there ahead."

"What, what daddy?"

"There's a four-leaf clover."

"Where daddy, where?" He points it out to her. "Can I pick it, daddy, or shall I leave it so next year there will be hundreds of four-leaf clovers?"

Daddy smiles, "No, darling, it's OK to pick it because next year

[116]

there just would be three-leaf clovers, which are what they usually are. Four-leaf clovers are special, just like you, princess. So pick it for good luck." And he puts it through the buttonhole of her coat.

She looks down at it happily.

"And pretty soon we'll come to a dandelion and you may pick that." And sure enough, they do, and sure enough, she does, and, "Here, I will show you something. I will hold the dandelion under your chin, right here under your chinny-chin-chin, and we will see what we will see. Hum, just as I thought. I see yellow on your chin. You like butter, that's what that means. You like butter."

She claps her hands with delight, "Oh daddy, you're such fun, I just love to go out with you, daddy! You're such fun, you're such fun!"

They have a lovely morning, and when they come back, it is time for lunch. They come in and daddy yells, "Mommy? Mommy, here we are, here we are, hungry as bears."

"Oh, read me the story of the Three Bears."

"Come on, princess! Again? I have read you that story so many times."

"But just once more, daddy."

"OK. First we'll eat our lunch and then I'll read your story, and then you can have your nap."

Mommy comes out of the kitchen and laughs, saying, "Well, welcome back, just in time for lunch."

The little girl looks at daddy and says, "NO."

And daddy says, "Well, honey, it's lunch time. Aren't you hungry?"

"I want a story."

Dad persists, "Is lunch ready, mommy?"

And mommy says, "Don't I get a kiss, honey?"

But her little girl turns her face away and hugs daddy's leg: "No."

Mommy says, "OK, maybe later."

Then daddy says, "Well, I'd like one." And he and mommy exchange a kiss. They go into the dining room and mommy comes in with three lunches which she puts down on the table.

Her little girl shouts, "Hurry up, mommy, hurry up, daddy's going to read me a story as soon as we finish."

"OK. May I stay and listen to the story, too?"

"Well no, that's just for daddy and me, mommy."

"Oh, I see. Well, what do YOU say, daddy? May I stay?"

And daddy replies, "I should think so. You're my queen, and this is my princess, and of course you may stay."

"Oh well, OK, mommy," sighs the little girl, "OK. I'm sorry."

"That's all right, honey, I understand. Sometimes I like to be alone with daddy, too."

"Oh."

Then Daddy exclaims, "I'm starving, how about you, princess?"

"I'm hungry too, daddy."

"Well, thank you, mommy," says daddy, "For bringing us lunch."

But princess turns her head away. "Well, come on, let's go to the table and all sit down. I want to sit next to daddy."

Mommy laughs and says, "Oh I see how it is, I see how it is."

Daddy laughs too, and says, "Well, I want my queen next to me, so please sit here beside me, mommy, and you can sit on my other side, princess."

"OK," she pouts, giving her mother a cross look, then turning her eyes adoringly on daddy.

Mommy says, "We have such nice carrots. Did you notice the nice carrots?"

No answer from her daughter, but daddy replies, "Yes, they look delicious. Eat your carrots, princess."

"I don't want any carrots. I hate carrots."

Mommy looks at daddy and says, "Do you hate carrots?"

And daddy says, "No, I like carrots. Do you hate carrots?"

And mommy replies, "No I like carrots. So let's just eat the princess' carrots." And so they divide up the carrots on the princess' plate and they each take half.

She looks from one to the other with big eyes and says, "Well you might leave me one or two." So they cheerfully scrape several back onto her plate. And lunch proceeds with lots of laughter, and lots of jokes, and lots of fun.

And when lunch is over mommy gets up and announces, "Nap time."

The little girl pouts, "I'm not going to nap."

"Well, princess," says her daddy, "if you're not going to nap then perhaps we will be too tired for our walk this afternoon."

"Oh, I'll nap daddy. I didn't say I wouldn't nap."

Mommy and daddy exchange an amused glance, and mommy walks off with the dishes.

Now it is time for the story and nap. The princess climbs on daddy's lap and puts her head gently against his chest. He holds her lightly in his arms while he turns the pages for the umpteenth time to the story of the Three Bears. When he gets to the part about

" . . . first she tries the BIG bed, that was Daddy Bear's bed," he says, "Now you say it, princess," and she begins to recite the story.

"And so Goldilocks first tested the great big bed. That was the Daddy Bear's bed. It was too HARD! So she gets out of it. And she says, 'I'll try the middle-sized bed,' that's the Mommy Bear's bed, but it was too SOFT! So Goldilocks jumped out of it, and then she tried the Baby Bear's bed, and that was JUST RIGHT."

"That was beautiful, princess."

The little girl adds, "The End. You forgot to say 'The End,' daddy."

"You're right! The End."

"Daddy, I love you so much."

Her daddy replies, "I'm very glad. I love you, too."

"Daddy, when I grow up I'm going to marry you."

Daddy looks at her, looks into her eyes, and says, "Princess, I'm already married. I'm married to mommy. She is my queen and I am her king, and you are our little princess."

"But when I grow up, daddy, I will be queen and you will be king, and mommy won't be there at all."

Daddy smiles: "No princess, when you grow up you will find a prince all your own who is not married. And you and he will become king and queen of your own kingdom. And daddy and mama will be very very proud of you. And you can have your own princes and princesses."

"No, daddy, I am going to marry you. I don't want any old stranger prince. I want you."

Daddy gives her a big hug and says, "You know that's absurd, princess, don't you?" And he begins to tease her. She buries her face in his chest and listens, but says nothing.

Then she begins to giggle, and daddy says, "That's my big girl."

And that is the end of the episode.

Goldilocks

This is a story about a little girl and her daddy. She begs her daddy to read a story and he says, "OK, pudd n'. What story would you like?"

And she says, "Oh, daddy, read me Goldilocks and the Three Bears."

Her mommy says, "But, honey, you have heard that story at least a dozen times this week."

"Please, daddy," she says, ignoring her mother, "Please, daddy, read me Goldilocks." He sighs wearily, but says, "OK, sugar, go get the book out of the bookcase." She runs quickly, and pulls the book out of the case, comes back, climbs up on his lap, snuggles down in the crook of his arm, and looks at the page as he starts to read. She listens contentedly, her attention wandering now and then. But it's OK. She knows the story very well and when he misses a sentence she corrects him. Then he gets to the place that really captures her attention. "Goldilocks goes into the bears' house, and there she sees three beds." At this point daddy stops and says, "You know this story by heart, princess. How about your reading it to me?"

Happily, she agrees, and tells the story word for word. When she finishes, daddy looks down at her and she looks up at daddy and says, "Oooooh, that is such a good story, daddy."

He laughs.

Mommy gets up and says, "Well, I'll see you two in a little while. I have to go now and get some things together."

As soon as mommy has gone out, the little girl snuggles up to her daddy, and says, "Daddy, when I grow up, please, will you marry me?"

And daddy says, "No, sugar, I'm already married."

[120]

"Oh," says she, pouting, "but when I grow up, THEN you can ask me to marry you."

"No, honey. When you grow up you will find your own special person who will become your husband. And then you will get married to someone you love very much and be very happy."

"I want to maaaarry yoooou, Daddy."

He looks at her, and he smiles, "You know that's silly."

She begins to giggle, and he giggles. He tweaks her nose, and gives her a light kiss on the top of her head and says, "Come on, honey, let's go to the park."

She runs eagerly to get her coat and put it on. She pulls down her hat to cover her ears, and holds her hand out to daddy. Daddy takes it happily as he winds his scarf around his neck. As they go down the hall, he says, "We're going for a little walk, OK?"

Mommy comes to the door and smiles and says, "Great, have a good time, you two. Goodbye darling," she says to her daughter, who shrugs and impatiently runs ahead yelling, "Come on daddy, come on," completely ignoring mommy.

Daddy takes her hand and says, "Bye, mom. Bye, darling," and his wife answers, "Goodbye, dear, have a good time."

"We'll be back soon."

Meanwhile his little daughter is standing impatiently at the door, pressing her nose against the glass, and shuffling her feet back and forth. Daddy catches up, takes her hand and together they go down the front steps to the sidewalk. Looking both ways, they follow the crosswalk to the other side where the park begins. His small daughter runs ahead. Daddy points out the flowers, telling her their names. Then he points out the trees, and tells her their names. She repeats the names after him. They have a great time. She finds a bright little pebble, picks it up and stuffs it into her pocket. And so they stroll, enjoying themselves, as she chatters and daddy smiles, keeping pace with her.

When they come to a bend in the path, daddy spots a friend just ahead of them. The two approach him, and daddy greets him. His friend asks, 'Oh, is this your little daughter?"

And daddy proudly replies, "Yes, this is my big girl."

His friend looks at her remarking, "You certainly are a pretty little girl."

She looks shyly down, and then looks at her daddy questionly.

Her daddy says, "You can say 'thank you,' dear."

She looks shyly at the stranger and says, "Thank you," primly.

[121]

Daddy's friend continues, "You're exactly the kind of little girl I have always wanted." She looks at him doubtfully, and looks at daddy, and daddy is still smiling, so she relaxes, and the friend adds, "As a matter of fact, you can just come along with me, and I can be your daddy."

She looks at him with alarm, and says, "Oh no, oh no."

Her daddy says, "No. Nobody can have my daughter. We cannot spare her."

His friend persists, "But you could come for a nice ride with me, and see what I have in my car for you."

She looks at him solemnly and she says, "Oh no, my daddy has told me NEVER to get in anybody's car unless my parents give me permission, and that I am not to take anything from anybody unless my parents tell me it's all right, even if you offer me candy."

Her daddy looks at her thoughtfully and says, "That's right, darling, that's absolutely right. You are to run home immediately and tell mommy and daddy."

His friend frowns at him and says, "Well, excuse my French! I was only joking, of course."

And daddy says, "Yes, of course. But sometimes little kids don't know when you are joking or when you mean it. I'm sure you can understand that."

"Oh sure, sure," his friend responds, looking somewhat embarrassed.

Then the little girl asks, "Do you have any candy?"

"Well, I do think I might happen to have a peppermint, but I don't suppose you like pepper . . . "

"Oh, yes I do, yes I do!" Then she looks at daddy and asks, "If I don't get in his car, is it all right if I take his candy?"

"Yes, it's all right so long as you're with mommy or daddy."

Daddy's friend is holding out a peppermint which she takes as she politely says, "Thank you very much. Was that all right, daddy?"

"That was lovely, dear."

Soon after that they say "goodbye" and they go on with their walk.

When they come to the end of the path, daddy says, "Well, darling, it's time to turn around and head for home."

But she protests, "Aw, daddy, let's walk just a little bit more. It is such fun."

"Well, we have quite a walk just to get back to the house. So let's turn around. Oh! And I know what! Let's see if we can keep in step with each other. Let's go, right, left, right, left, right, left." Soon she joins the game, and they have a fine gigging time. Sometimes she pretends to get out of step, and then rushes to get back in step, and sometimes daddy gets out of step and rushes to get back in step. So, having a good time playing the game of keeping in step, they get back to their house.

Daddy shouts, "OK, darling, we're home! What's for lunch?"

Mommy comes out and says, "Hi there, you two." She gives daddy a kiss. And then she bends down to give her daughter a hug, but her daughter turns away as though not noticing. She runs ahead to take off her coat and her hat, and to go into the dining room where the table is set for lunch.

And that's the end of the episode.

Jack and the Beanstalk

We see a sturdy little boy. He seems to be, oh, around the age of five. He looks familiar. And he's out walking with his daddy. They're on the way to the playground, and daddy is holding a ball. He's tossing it in the air and catching it. Every once in a while he tosses it to his little son who tries to catch it, but he misses more often than not. His daddy praises him, and laughs, and they have a good time.

Daddy is carrying two gloves, a little one for his son, and a big one for himself. They walk along merrily until they come to a playground where there is a cinder oblong just long enough for playing catch. Daddy positions himself at one end of the oblong and his son stands at the other. Daddy hands him the glove, puts on his own glove, and tosses the ball.

The boy tries very hard to catch it but he misses, runs scampering after it, laughs, picks it up and tosses it to his father. It falls a little short, but his father scrambles after it and scoops it up. They both shout with excitement. Then daddy tosses the ball again, and this time the little boy manages to catch it in his glove. His daddy applauds him, "That was just great, son, that was great!" And together they continue to practice catching and throwing the ball. The little boy is feeling very proud of himself, and his daddy is having a great time as well.

Then daddy throws the ball faster and harder than before. His little son scrambles to catch it, but misses, and it hits him squarely on the nose. He stumbles, trips, and falls hard with all his weight on both knees in the cinder path. He stays down with tears streaming, howling in pain. Daddy rushes over, picks him up and tries to brush him off. His nose and both knees are bleeding profusely.

Daddy scoops him up in his arms and carries him back to the house as fast as he can go, balancing the gloves and the ball and the little boy as best he can. All the while his son is screaming and struggling, trying to get away from him. Daddy leaps up the front steps two at a time and bursts through the door.

Mother has run into the hall already having heard the anguished screams of her son. She runs up to them: "Now whatever, whatever is the matter?"

The little boy cries, "Mommy, mommy," and holds out his arms.

She takes him and says, "Now let's see. What is the trouble?"

Daddy explains while the little boy howls, "Mommy, mommy, mommy."

She carries him into the bathroom, sits down with him on her lap and calmly says, "Now let me have a little look and see what's the problem here." He is holding onto her with both hands and sobbing with his face buried in her bosom. She says, "Well, well, let me see. I don't think that this is too bad. But I believe it hurts a lot, honey, doesn't it? I'm sorry it hurts you this very much. But let's see if I can clean it up and make you more comfortable, OK?"

While he keeps on hollering and yelling louder and louder, mommy gently, very gently applies a cold cloth to the bloody little nose, and carefully, patiently, cleans the cinders out of the wounds. Then lightly she puts antiseptic on his knees, saying, "This may sting a little, darling, but it will keep you from getting an infection."

"No," he hollers, "Nooooo, that hurrrrts."

"Well, it's OK, honey, it's all over now. I know it hurts, and I am so sorry." She carries him then into his room, just as though he were a little baby again. She sits down in the rocker and cuddles him in her lap. His sobs begin to subside a little. He leans his head on her breast as she holds him. Soon he stops sobbing and hiccups a little from time to time. He murmurs, "Read me a story, mommy."

"OK, honey, what story would you like?"

"Read Jack and the Beanstalk, mommy."

Still holding him, she finds the storybook and starts to read. Her son snuggles closer and follows the familiar story dreamily. When the giant roars, "Fe, fi, fo, fum, I smell the blood of an Englishman. Be he live or be he dead, I'll grind his bones to make my bread!" the little boy shudders and presses even closer. And when she reads the part

[125]

where the giant's wife helps Jack escape, he smiles a little. Then, at last, when Jack chops down the beanstalk, the little boy's eyes close and he drops off to sleep.

She puts him to bed, covers him lightly with a soft blanket, and tiptoes away. He has a nice nap.

When he wakes his mommy is there waiting. He holds out his arms to her just as he did when he was a little fellow. She picks him up and carries him just as she did when he was a baby, and she holds him on her lap.

He looks at her and he smiles a little, and he says, "I love you, mommy," and she looks down into his eyes and says, "I love you too, darling."

And that's the end of the episode.

Latency

Softball

This story is about a little boy who looks very familiar to you. It's almost as if you know this boy. He is running noisily down the stairs to the front hall. He passes the kitchen door, and his mother calls out, "Whooooa there, where are you off to without your breakfast?"

"Aw, mom, listen, I'm late already. The gang is meeting in the schoolyard. We're having a softball game And I'm the pitcher. I have to be there!"

"Well, now, pitchers have to have fuel, so you just come in here. Your breakfast is ready. Here it is. Sit down and eat your breakfast, honey."

"Oh, mom, you don't understand. They can't start the game till I get there."

"I do understand. So, let's compromise."

"What do you mean?"

"Well, eat half your breakfast, how's that?"

"OK, all right. Gee, mom." Their eyes meet. Then he smiles at her, in spite of himself . . . the sweetest smile. She goes over to him, musses up his hair, and hugs him to her He puts his arm around her and he says, "You know mom, you really are cool."

She looks down at him and says, "OK, that makes two of us." He laughs, sits down and stuffs his breakfast down as fast as he can. His mother stands there looking at him, saying, "Oink, oink, oink." He laughs.

Then like a shot, he's out the door and running down the street, fleet as a deer, hugging his glove and his bat to his chest as he runs.

He gets to the school yard, races through the gate and yells, "Hi, fellas!"

They turn around yelling, "Hi ya."

He slows down and saunters over to them with the best imitation he can manage of a big ballplayer's macho gait. He takes up his position on the mound, looks around, and growls out of the corner of his mouth, "Well, what are we waitin' for? PLAY BALL!"

All the other boys yell, "Play ball."

The first batter is up and the kid pitches the ball. The umpire yells, "Baaall ONE!" He rubs his toe in the dust and polishes the ball, spits in his glove, winds up, and throws one fast and hard. "STRIKE ONE!" They are off and playing!

Between innings, as they stand around leaning on their bats and wiping the sweat out of their eyes, they see four girls come into the schoolyard. The girls go over near the steps to jump rope. The boys begin talking louder and pushing each other. The girls look down their noses, pretending to ignore them. In a stage whisper they say, "Boys are disgusting!" They go on whispering to each other, casting disdainful looks over at the boys on the field. The boys act tough and laugh too loud and slap each other on the back.

And that is the way the morning plays out. Too soon it's time for lunch. And our little kid says to his pals, "Are we going to play again or what are we gonna do?"

And the others say, "Why don't we go on over and swim this afternoon?"

"Oh, neat. What time are you going?"

"Oh, we thought we'd go around 1:30."

"OK, I'll meetcha. So long, gang."

They yell, "So long."

He runs off to his house, bangs through the front door, slams it shut, and yells, "I'm home, ma."

She comes to the kitchen door. "So I hear, so I hear, son. Go on, wash up. I have something special for lunch."

"Oh, great, I'm starving."

"I guess you are. Go on, wash up and come back in here. I have something you really like." She smiles fondly at him, and he grins at her.

He rushes up the hall and bumps smack into his dad. His dad says, "Whoa, there! Where are you off to in such a hurry?"

"Oh, I have to wash up for lunch. I'm hungry! You hungry, dad? Let's go eat lunch."

"Sure, that's fine."

His kid adds, "Mom says she fixed something real special. She's neat, isn't she, dad? She's really neat. I just figure she's about the neatest girl I know."

His dad smiles at him and says, "That's right, son, she is the neatest girl I ever knew."

His son looks at him speculatively, then turns away, goes to the bathroom to wash his whole face and run the water through his hair and scrub his hands, and then races noisily down to get his lunch.

And that is the end of the story.

Girl Friends

This is a story about a young girl. There is a house which looks rather familiar to you. Up the front walk three girls arrive. They are perhaps 8 years old. They are strolling up the walk giggling and talking to each other. One comes up close to the house and, looking up at a second story window, she calls, "Yoo-hoo, yoo-hoo! Can you come out to play? Yoo-hoo."

The window is raised and a young girl sticks her head out, "Hi! What you all gonna do?"

The one under the window shouts up, "We thought we'd go down to the schoolyard and fool around. Wanna come?"

"Just a minute. I'll have to ask my mom. I'll be right down." She dashes down, races into the kitchen and breathlessly asks her mom, "Can I go to the schoolyard, mom, my friends are here. Can I, can I, can I? Mom, mom, can I?"

Her mother turns around, smiling at her and says, "Yes, if you promise to be back at 11:30 because that's lunch time, you know."

Her daughter protests, "Oh, lunch. They don't have to go home for lunch."

Her mother raises one eyebrow at her and says, "Are you sure?"

And her daughter replies, "Why don't you fix me some lunch? I can take a sandwich, then I don't have to come racing home for any ole lunch."

Her mother asks, "Do you think the others have their lunches?"

"Oh sure, they always take their lunch."

"Are you sure?" her mother repeats.

"Well, no, I'll go ask."

She runs out and asks, "Did you all bring sandwiches? Are you going to have lunch in the schoolyard?"

The others chorus, "Oh, rats, no. We have to go home for lunch."

"Oh!"

She runs back into the house and says, "Well, they don't have any sandwiches so I guess we'll all have to go home for lunch."

Her mother looks at her thoughtfully, "I have an idea."

"Oh, mom, I'm late. They're waiting for me."

"But I have a good idea."

"Yeah, I know, I know."

But her mother persists, "Well, would you like to hear my idea or not?"

"Really, mom, you know your ideas are sometimes not so great."

Looking steadily at her daughter she says, "Well, I was going to suggest you bring them back here and we have a lunch party."

"Oooh, mom. Wait, I'll ask 'em." She runs outside and asks them if they would like to come to her house for lunch. They could have a party at 11:30.

"Oh, yeah," they shout, then one of the group groans, "Oooh, my mom always says no, she's so out of it."

The others say, "Well we could call up and just . . . I know, let's go call our moms now." They troop into the house. The young girl's mother watches them with a twinkle in her eye. One by one they call their mothers, and the message is the same, "Mom, I've been invited for lunch. Yeah, yeah, I'm invited for lunch. Can I, can I? Well, mom, everybody else is staying for lunch. OK, mom. Thanks, mom." Each one repeats the same formula. They all get permission.

And as they run out the door, at the very last minute, her daughter turns and calls, "Thanks, mom. We'll be here at 11:30."

They race down to the schoolyard, giggling, and whispering, sharing secrets, walking with their hands linked together, having a wonderful time. As they approach the schoolyard, they see a teacher walking up the path before them. Nudging each other, they smirk, and then they whisper to each other. They all laugh and giggle. It's obvious that they are making very unfriendly comments about the teacher. Then one of them imitates her walk and the others squeal with laughter. They're having a great time.

They see, out of the corner of their eyes, a group of boys playing a game of softball. They whisper, and then they sneer. They nudge each other. They walk over to the school steps and sit down. They are having a fine time, laughing and talking and enjoying each other.

[133]

All of a sudden, right in the middle of their huddle, a softball lands, kersplatt! Well, the little girls are outraged. They turn and look down their noses at the "nasty boys" exclaiming to each other, "Isn't that just like a nasty boy? Look at how dirty they are! Disgusting! Phew, smelly too! Dirty!"

Then to the boy approaching to retrieve his ball, they say, "Well, can't you look where you're throwing your dirty old ball?"

The young boy sneers back, "Oh, yeah, sissy prissy has a tizzy."

The girls answer in unison, "Sticks and stones can break my bones but names can never hurt me."

Now all the boys are hitting each other, pushing each other, and guffawing. The girls are sneering, turning their noses up, and acting just as prissy as the young boy said.

Finally, one of the girls says, "Well here, take your ole ball," and she tries to throw it to them, but it falls far short.

The boys guffaw and sneer, "Just like a girl. Can't even throw a ball. You throw a ball like a girl!"

The girls all sit up straight, turn their heads away, turning their backs to the boys and pretending not to notice them anymore.

Suddenly, one of the young girls says, "Uh oh, look at the clock up there." It's 11:30 already. They hastily jump up and, as fast as they can go, they race back to the house to have their lunch party. They bang into the house, actually as sweaty as the boys by this time.

As they troop in, mother looks at them and says, "Well, the bathroom is down the hall to the right, and the soap is in the dish, so when you have cleaned up those little paws, come back here."

"Mother," exclaims her daughter, "really . . . little paws! I really think that's tacky, mother. Tacky!"

"Oh, I beg your pardon," mother apologizes, smiling at her. "Your dirty little hands is what I should say."

"Oh, really, mother, *really*! Come on," she beckons to the others as they go down to the bathroom. There they immediately start giggling as they wash their hands.

When they come back, mother says, "The table is in here. Please do sit down. Your lunch is ready." She serves an especially nice lunch for which very little thanks are forthcoming. The girls are too busy whispering, talking and telling secrets again.

At last, one of them remembers her manners, and says, "Thank you very much."

Mother replies, "You're very welcome, dear. I'm glad you enjoyed it."

Then the others chime in belatedly.

When their lunch is finished, they carefully put their folded napkins back on the table, all but the young girl who lives there. She simply lets it drop. It lands on the seat of her chair as she marches out the door.

Her mother calls, "Where are you going, dear?"

"Really, mother, I'm not going anywhere. I'm just going outside for a little while with my friends. Do you mind?"

Her mother smiles, "No, I don't mind but I do like to be told where you're going and that's the rule, as you know."

"Oh," complains the young girl, whispering to her friends, "Rules, rules, rules, rules, rules." And out the door they go.

Once outside they begin asking each other what they would like to do. After hemming and hawing, one of them suggests swimming. The others enthusiastically agree. They separate, each racing to her own house to get permission and pick up swimsuits.

Our young girl rushes back into the house shouting, "Mom, mom, we're going swimming! Can I? Can I? Everyone else is going, mom!"

Her mother appears in the hallway, smiles, and says, "I think that's a good idea, if you will wait an hour before going in. Promise?"

"Sure, OK," and then, under her breath, "Rules, rules, rules" Out loud she says, "Have to run! Bye, mom!"

And that is the end of this episode.

Tuna Fish

This story takes place in the kitchen. Mother is defending her
lunch menu, and her daughter, who seems to be about 9 years
old, says, "Well, it just seems to me that with all those cook-
books you have, you'd be able to find something besides tuna fish for
lunch three times a week."

"Now, come on," protests her mom, "You know I don't fix tuna
fish three times a week."

"Well then, two times a week."

"OK, OK, supposing you just eat it now and I'll see what I can do
tomorrow. How would you like chowder tomorrow?"

"Yuck," retorts her daughter, "Is that all you can think of?"

Then her mother bristles, "Look here, missy, if you don't like the
menu around here, supposing you compose one and I'll be happy to
oblige."

"Humpf," answers her daughter, picking at her tuna fish with a
limp wrist, but managing somehow to finish it.

At this point her father comes in and remarks, "Well, I see we've
finished lunch here."

Mother says, "Yes, dear, would you like some? There is more here."

"I don't mind if I do."

As he sits down his daughter says, "You don't seem to mind having
tuna fish three times a week."

Her mother gives her a warning glance as her father says, "I
haven't had it three times this week. Have you had it three times this
week, mom?"

And mom says, "No, I haven't had it three times this week."

"Well," looking at his daughter, "It seems extraordinary to me that

[136]

you're the only one in the family who had tuna fish three times this week. You must have been doing some cooking on the side."

The young girl pouts, "Oh, dad, that isn't funny. You just think you're funny but you're not very funny."

"Well," he says with mock earnestness, "I guess I haven't got a big reputation as a stand-up comic."

The little girl sulks, looks at them, stands up and says in a haughty voice, "Well, I suppose I may be excused now, if you don't mind."

Her parents look at each other, grin, and say, "We actually do not mind in the least."

She exits, looking back over her shoulder disapprovingly at them as she marches out muttering to herself, "They really should shape up. They really need to shape up." And she goes up to her room.

That is the end of this story.

Puberty

Masturbation

This is a story about a young boy. He's standing eagerly at the front door. It's evening and he's watching and waiting for someone. Suddenly his body straightens up and he opens the door. There's a big smile on his face as he says eagerly, "Hi, dad."

His dad comes bounding up the steps, gives his son a bear hug, and says, "How are you doing son? Did you have a good day?"

"Yeah, dad, it was fine. I was, um, kinda waitin' for you to get home."

"Oh? Something special?"

"Well, no, I was just remembering a couple of talks we've been having and I've been kinda thinkin' about them."

"Well, OK, son. Just let me get my coat off. Give me time to go in and say hello to your mom back there, and then . . . maybe before dinner, after dinner, what do you think?"

"Well . . . mmmaybe after dinner, dad."

"Do you think you can wait that long?" And they both laugh. He goes in to greet his wife while his son stands hanging around the door and grinning.

His mom looks over and says, "Got something special for you tonight at dinner."

Her son beams and says, "Shall I guess?"

And she says, "Sure."

So he says, "Ummm, a steak and baked potatoes."

"Nope."

He says, "Hamburger?"

"Nope."

"OK, I give up."

His dad goes over to the stove, looks in the pot, and says, "Mmm mmmm, don't tell! This will be a surprise."

Then the boy says, "Let's see if I can guess by smelling it." And then . . . "Mom! It isn't!"

She says, "What do you think?"

He says, "It isn't."

She says, "Yep, it is!"

"Oh boy, spaghetti!"

He goes over to her, puts his arms around her, squeezes her hard, and she squeals, "Hey! Hey! You don't know your own strength!"

When they all sit down to dinner there is a lot of pleasantry, a lot of laughter, and when dinner is cleared away, they go into what looks like dad's study.

And dad says to mom, "Will you excuse us, we have a little men's talk about to go on here."

She looks at him, and laughs. "Of course, just let me know when it's OK for the women to join in." And she leaves.

Dad sits down in his big chair. His son sits on a low stool very close to his knees, leans his arm on his dad's chair, and props his chin up on his fist. Dad says, "OK, let's have it."

"Well, dad, um, you know after we talked a little bit, I've been thinkin' about some things. It's a little hard for me to ask you about 'em, but, uh, I'm interested in some things, um, well, you know. . . . What do you think about masturbating, dad?"

His dad asks, "What do you mean, what do I think?"

"Well, I don't know, you hear so many things, you know. You hear really stupid things."

His father laughs, and he says, "Yes, I know, I think I've heard a few."

And his son says, "Yeah, you know, you hear that if you masturbate you could go crazy, and you can, maybe, hurt yourself. You know, that kind of stuff."

And his father laughs, "Yes, I know, but actually masturbating is a very private affair."

"Yeah, that's right."

And dad says, "Yes, masturbating is not something you want to do in public, and it's not particularly dinner-table conversation. And also, it's not much of a joke."

"How do you mean that, dad?"

"Well, a lot of people like to make a big heehaw joke out of sex, but although sex is play and is enjoyable, it's not really a horseplay kind of subject for cheap jokes."

[142]

"I know what you mean, dad. But, you know, sometimes I think when you get with the guys and you feel embarrassed, the only way you can cover up your embarrassment is to make some kind of a silly joke."

"Yes, I can buy that. That's right, I buy that."

"But what do you think, dad? Do you think it's a bad thing to do?"

His father looks at him earnestly, and says, "I do not think it's a bad thing to do. I think it's a very natural thing to do, and that very often we need to have some release of physical tensions, sexual tensions. And, right now, you're approaching a very, very sexual period in your life. In our society, in our culture, it isn't appropriate, nor do we encourage very young people to indulge in sex, because there are all kinds of difficulties and things that maybe we'll talk about sometime soon."

"Oh, would ya, dad? I sure would like to hear what you think about it, because I hear so much stuff, you know, you hear so much . . . well, if you'll excuse me . . . just crap."

His father smiles and says, "That's right. You hear a lot of crap about it."

"So would you tell me straight, dad? Is it OK to masturbate?"

"You tell me one thing first, before I tell you what I think. How do you feel about yourself when you masturbate?"

"To tell you the truth, while I'm masturbating, I feel great, and when I'm finished, you know, I feel wonderful. But after that I begin to think about myself and I think, 'Well, gosh, is this something, you know, like could this be a sin?' And I begin to feel like I'm kinda guilty or something."

His father smiles at him and strokes his hair. "Well, son, it's very natural for a healthy young animal to need to have sexual release, and masturbating is perfectly healthy and natural as long as you don't impose it on other people, and as long as you understand that this is just a part of your sexual life. It plays a useful part, especially in our society where the sex act is a long-postponed experience—longer, for instance, than in some other cultures where sometimes the young people are married as young as 13 or 14."

"Oh, I see, dad, well, gee, that helps me out."

"But never worry about it being injurious to you, son, because it is a very natural activity, and is really OK as long as, like with everything else, you do it in moderation."

"OK, dad, that sounds like pretty good advice, but how do I know when it's in moderation?"

His father smiles at him and says, "When it feels like it's too much, it's too much. And when it feels like it's too little, it's too little. And that's how you know." With this he makes a fist and punches his son lightly on the upper arm.

"Gee dad, that really does help me. And there are some things I want to ask you about, but I really gotta do my homework now, so thanks a lot, dad."

His father smiles, chuckles, and says, "Tell your mom it's time for the females to join the males."

And that's the end of the episode.

Pubic Hair

This is a story about a boy who is sitting on a bench with his dad. They look fairly familiar to you, both the boy and the father. The park around them is very lovely. The day is mild and pleasant.

The young boy turns to his father and says, "Dad, I don't know how to talk about this to you. It's kinda hard," and he gets red up to the roots of his hair.

His father looks at him, smiles and says, "It's OK, son, take your time."

The boy smiles at him a little, gratefully, and says, "Well, um, I'm worried about something, dad."

His father says, "Mmmm?"

"Yeah, you know, I know you know, I'm 10 years old, and I'm starting to get hair down there, you know."

His father looks at him and says, "You mean pubic hair?"

And the young boy says, "Yeah, and I look at the other boys in the locker room. Nobody else has pubic hair, dad."

"Well, boys start that at very different ages, and 10 is quite young, but it's OK, you know. There's nothing wrong about it. It just shows that you're getting to be a man."

"Well, but, everybody else, they're still boys, dad. I felt funny, so I'll tell you what I did."

"Oh? What did you do?"

"Uhm, I shaved it off, dad."

His father smiles, and says, "That's OK, son, if you feel more secure doing that, there is nothing wrong with that. But there will come a day, son, when you're going to be very proud of having pubic hair, because it is very manly."

His son looks at him with big round eyes and says, "It is? You mean the guys won't make fun of me?"

"Well, I don't know. I don't know the guys, so I don't know what they'll do or how uncomfortable they might feel to see somebody else get ahead of them a little."

"Oh, is this getting ahead?"

His dad smiles at him and says, "Well, yes, son, I rather think so. You're starting a little earlier than most, but soon there will be others catching up with you. And pretty soon the guys who will be worried are the ones who don't start until they're well into their teens. They get really scared, sometimes, that there is something wrong with them. Of course, there isn't. It's just that we all have our own time clock. Earlier or later is equally good. We all develop in our own time, and usually it's fine. Usually we are perfectly normal."

"Well, gee, dad, thanks a lot, you know that helps me a lot. Hey, listen, I don't have to get undressed in front of those guys unless I want to."

His dad smiles at him and says, "Sure, but you know, son, I predict there'll be a time when you will want to because you'll feel good about being so far along."

"Well, gee, thanks, dad."

"There will be other changes, too, son. You will find that your penis will grow."

"Really?"

"Sure enough, it will start to grow larger. You will also find that your vocal cords, somewhere along the line, will begin to thicken, and you'll have a voice change. And that voice change often is embarrassing to kids who don't understand that it's a sure sign that they're getting a man's voice. When that change begins, sometimes when you talk, you'll start with your nice new deep voice that suddenly breaks in the middle, and you'll find yourself squeaking real high. And you'll be surprised, and perhaps self-conscious, but that's OK, because every boy changing into being a man experiences that."

"Gee, dad, I sure am gonna make some changes."

"Well, what did you think? After all, here you are in the last stages of being a little boy. How do you think you'll get to be a tall grown-up man?"

"Well, I guess I didn't think about it too much, dad."

"Oh . . . well, I guess that's pretty normal too, son. Why would you, especially if most of the kids around you are still young boys."

"Yeah, dad, that's rough, you know."

[146]

His dad looks at him, puts his arm around him, and with his hand on his son's shoulder, says, "Yes son, I guess it is." Then, looking at him and smiling he asks, "You think you can survive it?"

His son breaks into a sheepish smile, and says, "Yeah, I guess I'd rather it be this way than waiting until I'm 16 and worrying about it."

"And there is something else nice," his dad adds, "something very nice begins to happen as soon as you begin your puberty changes. Incidentally, that is what you are starting now, and that will go on through your teens as you develop into a full grown man. But soon now you will start, and I know you're going to like this, you're going to start to have a growth spurt. Pretty soon you're going to find yourself getting quite tall."

"Really, dad?"

"Yes, getting pubic hair signals that you have started a new growth cycle."

"Oh boy, gee dad, maybe I'll be able to make the basketball team."

His father grins at him and says, "There is no question that you will probably feel like trying out in a year or so."

"Oh, boy, dad, that's neat, dad. You know, that bothered me. . . . There are a lot of kids that are bigger than me."

"Oh sure, there always will be."

"Well, there are a couple who are smaller than me."

"Sure . . . there always will be. But now, you're going to experience getting taller and that's pretty nice."

"You bet," his son grins, "You bet."

"OK. Is there anything else?"

After a long pause, his son says, "Well, dad, uh, I'd, uh, like to ask you . . . how does a guy get to be strong, you know, real tough, and uh, know how to hold his own, you know? Sometimes I get mad and, uh, I get so mad that I don't think I can figure out what I really want to do. Sometimes I just get mad and fight, but that never gets me what I want."

"Oh, yeah, I know what you mean. You want to be able to show that you're angry without really hurting somebody else or hurting yourself. Is that what you're trying to say?"

And the kid answers, "Yeah, yeah, that's right, I don't want to get hurt, and I guess I really don't want to hurt the other guy, not that I can most of the time, dad. I am not the best fighter."

"Oh? Does that bother you son?"

"Well, yeah, it does, 'cause I figure I don't know how to hold my own, dad. I don't know how to be tough like the other guys."

[147]

"Oh! That's just an acquired skill. Let me see, let's see if some of these things would appeal to you. Uh, I happen to know about a wrestling class that's starting up."

"Oh, we've got one at school, dad."

"You have? How about for guys your age?"

"Well, yeah, there's some guys in my class that are wrestling. Would that help?"

"It might, if you like it. Yes, that's one way to learn how to take attack, and to attack, to play by the rules, and to learn how to defend yourself. Yeah, that's a very good thing."

"Well, maybe I could do that, dad."

"OK, how about investigating that at school, son? See if that would appeal to you. I think wrestling might answer your purposes for the time being."

"Gee, dad, I will."

After a moment, his father continues, "Then there are sports, you know. Learning to play soccer, for instance. That's a very good game, a very aggressive game. It teaches you to take the initiative and get in there. It also teaches you team spirit so you can work with other people. You can be very, very aggressive on the field and then find out that all of you can be friends afterwards. That's a wonderful lesson to learn."

"Well, I guess there will be soccer in the fall, dad. Maybe I'll go out and talk to the coach. Maybe I could play."

"That's good, that's very good. What other sports do they have at school?"

"Well, you know, there's basketball, and there's football. At least we fool around a little bit. We don't really play football yet, but we learn to make passes, and we kick the ball, and we learn to run."

"Well, all of that is very, very good. All of those games build muscles, and teach you not to be afraid to use your body, to express your feelings with your body. So I certainly think all the sports you're talking about are good."

"Well, there's this too. . . . What do you think, dad? Is it sissy to like music?"

His father looks at him sharply, and asks, "Sissy?"

"Well, I don't know, dad. A lot of the guys seem to think that if you like to sing, like the guy, you know, the guy who teaches the choir. . . . Well, he asked me to sing, but I was afraid the other guys would laugh at me. He says I have a good voice, dad. And you know something, I

[148]

wouldn't want the guys to know it, but . . . you know, I like to sing, and I really like music, dad."

"Well son, do you think that Pagliacci . . . you know we have his records . . . "

"Yeah."

"Do you think he's a sissy?"

"Well, no," his son replies thoughtfully, "I don't. But he's a big man. Can boys sing, and not be told to go play with the girls?"

"Is that what they tell you, son?"

"Well, not exactly, but that's what I'm afraid of."

"Well, who are the other guys in the choir?"

"Oh, I never thought about that."

"Then go hang around, and when they break up, figure out if you think they are sissies who ought to go play with girls. Maybe you'll find some friends there. They are singers like you."

"Oh, boy, dad, that's a wonderful idea."

And with that, he turns, slumps down on the park bench, spreads his legs out straight with his heels down, his toes pointing up, and his arms behind his head.

His dad looks at him, smiles and says, "Sure is a lovely day, isn't it, son?"

And his son murmurs, "Mm-hmm."

And that is the end of this episode.

Woman Talk

This story is about a young girl who looks very familiar to you. The young girl is running up the walk carrying her school books. She bursts through the front door, and she calls, "Mom? Mom! Mom, where are you?"

Her mother pokes her head out of the sitting room doorway and says, "Here I am darling, in here. What is it?"

"I'm home! What are you doing?"

"I was just getting a few papers together. What is it?"

"Well," the young girl pauses at the threshold of the room, looks at her mother uncertainly, "I don't know, mom, um, it's just something at school. I really would like to talk to you a little bit. OK?"

Her mom settles herself back in her chair, and says, "Of course, honey, it's OK. Come, sit over here near me, and tell me what's on your mind."

The young girl comes into the room, and sits down on the little footstool near her mom. She clasps her knees with her two hands and rocks back and forth a few moments, while her mother sits quietly looking at her, completely attentive. "You know, mom, they have these health classes, you know, where they tell you about . . . " and then she giggles, and makes the sign for quotes with her fingers in the air, " . . . you know, quote, 'facts of life,' unquote."

Her mother laughs and says, "Yes, I know about them, honey."

"Well, mom, there's some questions I have, but you know they give these facts of life not just to the girls, but the boys are there, too, and I don't feel like asking questions because I feel very self-conscious asking questions. So, I thought maybe I'd ask you some questions

[150]

because when I ask my friends, everybody has a different idea. So I thought maybe I could talk it over with you."

"By all means, honey. Anyway I can help, or anything I can offer, you know I'm happy to do that."

"Uh, first of all, mom, I need to know about this, um, monthly period bit."

"Oh, you mean menstruation? Why don't you tell me what you know, because it's been a long time since I've been in school and learned about this. You probably know more about it than I, darling."

"I just know what they told me, mom. But I don't feel really comfortable asking questions there like I do with you."

Her mother smiles pleasantly at her and says, "So tell me what you know, and then fire away with questions."

"Well, I know that we have a uterus, and that's where babies grow. And I know that we have two fallooop . . . fallopian . . . yes, fallopian tubes, and that's where the eggs travel all the way down to the uterus. Then one egg is deposited per month, first through one tube, and then the other tube the next month. And the little egg fastens itself to the wall of the uterus, but if there is no sperm, it doesn't fasten itself, since it hasn't united with the sperm. And so it just goes on out of the body, and so does all the good rich blood that has been stored up for the whole month hoping for a fertilized egg to attach itself to the wall of the uterus. The blood is to nourish a fertilized egg."

"Oh," exclaims her mother, "You really have learned your lesson well, darling."

"It's so *interesting*, mom. And then it all goes through an opening called the cervix when the uterus discards the unfertilized egg and the blood. That is called menstruation. Usually it lasts from two or three days to five or six days, depending on the person. How long do you menstruate, mom?"

Her mother looks at her, then smiles and says, "Usually there is heavy blood flow for three days, and then much less. Usually by five days it is through."

"Oh, so do you think that's how I will menstruate too, mom?"

"Most likely, I think. But I do hear that some young women have a much heavier flow for a much shorter time, so that might be your experience, or it might be the opposite. It's hard to tell."

"How old were you mom, when you started?"

Her mother smiles at her, then replies, "I started rather young. I was 11."

[151]

"Oh, that's what I am! Do you think I'll start soon, mom? Do you?"

"I wouldn't be surprised."

"You see, mom, um, some of the girls, some of my friends. . . . Betsy is already getting her period, I understand, although she didn't tell me so, and others say that Ruthie is, too. And here I am. I'm 11 years old! You can tell, you know, I'm already starting to sprout bosoms."

Her mother laughs and says, "Yes, I noticed."

"And I also have some hair starting, mom."

And her mom says, "Yes. Well, it's the right time."

"Say mom, could I have a bra?"

Her mother laughs and says, "I don't know. Do you think you really need one?"

"Gee, I don't think I really, really need one, but a lot of the girls are wearing them."

"Oh, I see. Maybe we could get you a double A or a triple A or something like that if you'd like to have one. It's OK. I don't see any reason why you shouldn't."

"OK!" Her daughter smiles happily, and her mom adds, "So, would you like to go and buy it, or do you want me to buy it, or shall we go together?"

"Oh, you buy it, mom. I don't think . . . I don't want to go and buy it. Maybe I'll buy it next time."

"Sure, OK. Next time I get to the store I'll get you one."

"Well, then, there is still this business about when do you think I'm going to get my period, mom?"

Her mother looks at her thoughtfully and says, "You know, ordinarily it's usual to get it any time between the ages of 10 and 15. Most young girls get it at 12 or 13, I'm given to understand, but it's OK to get it sooner and its OK to get it later. It doesn't mean anything . . . at what age you get it."

"Am I gonna have to wait two whole years?"

Her mother smiles. "Perhaps, and perhaps not. It just depends on how your body develops, dear. And it isn't better to start at 11 than at 12 or 13, and it isn't better at 13 than at 12 or 11, or later, or earlier. It has nothing to do with good or better. It's just the way that your body makes itself ready."

"OK . . . but, mom, isn't it messy? I hear it's awfully messy. The girls tell me at school that they hate it. And do you know what some of them call it, mom?"

"What?"

"The curse. It's supposed to be a curse on women."

Her mother laughs easily and says, "Nonsense. There is no curse on women. That's just an old folk tale left over from when people were superstitious. And anyway, I don't think that's a woman's idea."

"So, whose idea is it then, mom?"

"Well, I think that's sort of a man's idea."

"Oh, why is that, mom? Why is that? Why would men think that?"

"I'm not really sure, but it has something to do with superstition, and the idea that a woman is unclean at that time. But that is really nonsense. It is good clean blood, special blood for a little life to nourish itself with. So how could it be unclean? It is NOT unclean. It's good healthy blood."

"Oh, yes, that really makes sense to me, mom." She pauses for a moment and then asks, "Oh, well, mom. If I should get it, what would I do? A lot of girls wear tampons."

"Let's talk about that, dear. Did you know that you have a special little membrane there in your vagina?"

"No, they didn't tell me that."

"Well, yes, there's a little membrane. It's called the hymen."

"Oh that's a funny name."

"What's funny about it?"

"Oh, I don't know, hi-man, high men, it should be hy-woman."

"Oh, you are funny," laughs her mom, "You sound like a feminist."

"I sort of am, mom. Is that wrong?"

"No indeed, no indeed, that's very much all right. That membrane is near the opening, below the cervix."

"Oh, I know about the cervix, that's where the baby comes out."

"That's right. Tampons sometimes are difficult to use because of the hymen. So, we'll see. And if you like, I can buy you some sanitary napkins, and they can be here just for you. . . . Would you like that? And I'll show you where they are, and if you should start to get your period when I'm not here, you'll have some."

"Do you think I could do it by myself, mom?"

Her mother laughs reassuringly, "I'm certain you could do it by yourself. You're not going to want to have somebody do that for you. It's not very complicated and I'm sure you'll do it very well."

"Oh, gosh, that's nice mom. Thanks, mom. Thanks a lot. Those were a lot of the questions I didn't really want to ask in my sex education class. With all those boys!"

"I can understand that," her mom replies, "I can understand that. That's not what you would really want, woman talk, in front of young boys. I understand. So it's all right to ask me, and it's all right to talk about it with your friends. And it is also very much all right to check it out if something sounds weird to you, or very different from what we've said. OK?"

"OK."

Her mother takes her into her arms and gives her a big hug.

After a short pause, her daughter says, "This business, you know, mom, about intercourse."

Her mom looks at her attentively and asks, "Yes?"

"Well, um, I know what they do and all, but that just seems so horrible to me! I don't think I would like that, mom."

"No, you wouldn't like it, honey, unless it's with someone whom you love. But when it's with someone you love, like your husband, it's very, very enjoyable."

Then, thoughtfully, "I don't think you need worry about that yet, because that is really some time away, and you haven't, that I know of, begun to feel much attraction for the opposite sex."

"Uh, mom, to be honest, I really have."

Her mother raises her eyebrows. "Oh, you have?"

"Well, sure, but I haven't done anything about it, of course."

Her mother smiles.

"But, umm, you know Jimmy?"

Her mother nods, "Sure, I've known Jimmy since he was a baby."

"Don't you think he's kinda nice, Mom?"

"Yes, I do. I think he's very nice."

"Well, you know, he hangs around a little after school, and sometimes we walk home part of the way together. Ummm, he is nice, mom. I have to say though, mom, he's funny, because the minute some other boy comes in sight he acts like he isn't with me. I'll be talking to him one minute, and the next minute he isn't there."

Her mother laughs, and says, "Young boys get embarrassed just like young girls."

"Oh, I see. Well, mom, I do think he's very nice, but I don't know exactly what to do about it."

And her mother looks at her, "What would you like to do about it, honey?"

"I don't know, um . . . um . . . I don't know. What do you do? What is the next step? Do you just go on walking home together, and then have him disappear whenever any other boys come along?"

Her mother laughs, "I don't think he'll keep on disappearing for very long, but I suggest that you keep on acting toward Jimmy the way you always have—like you think he's a very nice young boy, and that you like him very much, and that you want to be friends."

"Oh, is that all?"

"That's quite a lot, honey, quite a lot. But if you can remember to do that, I think you won't have a very hard time knowing what to do next."

Just then there are voices outside, young girls' voices, and they are calling, "Can you come out? Hey, can you come out and play?"

The young girl jumps up quickly, gives her mother a quick kiss on the cheek, and says, "Gotta go. Bye, mom." And she rushes out the front door.

And that's the end of this episode.

First Menstruation

This is a story about a young girl. She appears to be 11, 12, or perhaps even 13 years old. She looks very familiar to you.

She runs up the walk, slams the front door behind her, and runs to her bedroom. Then picking up the telephone, she dials a number. When someone answers, she asks, "Uh, is my mother there? . . . Oh, well . . . do you expect her? Oh, OK, thank you."

She hangs up, looking disappointed, and then sits down, reaches for a magazine, thumbs through it, but her mind is not on it. Restlessly, she gets up and walks to the window. She peers through the curtains, comes back and sits down. She picks up the magazine again, then throws it on the floor. She jumps up and hurries to the front door. Opening it she peers up the street, first to her right, then to her left. She is very restless, very upset, and very eager to see her mother. Finally a car pulls into the driveway. She hears the motor turn off. She looks out to see her mother getting out of the car, slamming the door behind her.

Flinging the front door open, she calls, "Mom, mom." Her mother looks up, surprised. "Oh, I'm so glad you're home!"

Her mother asks anxiously, "What is the matter, honey? What's happened? What's wrong?"

Her daughter cries, "Hurry, mom, please come in. Please hurry up."

Her mother comes in hastily, puts down the grocery bags she's carrying, slips out of her coat, turns to her daughter, and asks, "What is it, honey? Come here." She holds her by the shoulders, and looks into her face. "Whatever is going on?"

[156]

Her daughter pulls her by the hand, crying, "Come sit down with me, mom. I . . . I need to talk to you."

Her mom anxiously replies, "Well, of course, dear, of course." They go into the sitting room and she sits down in her favorite armchair.

Her daughter sits in another chair pulled up close so that their knees are almost touching, as she says, "Guess what?

"What? I can't imagine. What?"

"Well," her daughter hesitates, "Now that I can talk about it, I don't know how to begin."

"It's OK, honey. Begin at the beginning." She looks at her daughter intently, searching out her eyes with tenderness and concern.

"Oh, moooom! I got it!"

"You got it? You got what?"

"Moooom, I started my period today, and I didn't know where you were."

"Oh, so that's it," relieved. "Let me put my arm around you. Come on, come over here. OK, now tell me about it."

"Oh, ma, I felt so funny. I really felt funny."

"Uh huh."

"So I went to the bathroom and I looked and sure enough it had started."

"Oh? And where were you, honey?"

"I was at school, mom, and I didn't know what to do."

"I can see how that would be uncomfortable, dear. What did you do?"

"I went up to the teacher and I said I wasn't feeling well, and she said to go report to the nurse, so I did. And I didn't know what to say to the nurse. I thought she would laugh at me acting like such a ninny, because I felt like crying, so I went down the hall."

"Uh huh . . . and when you went down the hall, did you find the nurse?"

"Yeah. She was busy, so I sat there, and I was afraid, you know, that maybe it would show on my skirt, and so I crossed my legs and hoped."

"Yes?"

"Finally she got to me and she said, 'What seems to be the trouble?' And I told her, 'I started my period and I don't have anything with me, and I want to go home.' She smiled at me and said, 'I can understand that. But I can give you something, and then you can go home more comfortably.' So she brought out this pad, and she gave it to me, and she explained how I stick it on my panties, and then I could just walk home and everything would be fine. So I said 'Thank you' and she wrapped it in a little envelope for me. She's really nice, mom. But all the time I felt so funny. I really felt funny. I don't know why I felt so scared, mom, but I just felt scared."

"I really do understand. You see, I know how you feel. Remember, I, too, had that happen to me for the first time, and I remember very well how I felt and, you know, it was very much the same way you feel. Not too different."

"Really mom? I'm not just a ninny? The other girls don't talk about crying and feeling scared."

"Well, honey, maybe they just don't like to admit it. But I really don't think it's so unusual."

"Oh, mom."

"Now tell me about it."

"Mom, I just feel so funny."

"Tell me how funny you feel."

"Well, I just feel like now I'm going to be different, and I don't know how I'll be, if I'm different."

"Oh ... I don't think you are going to be THAT different, you know."

"You're sure? Because now I'm getting my period I'm afraid I'll be very different. Will I have to be a grown-up right away?"

Her mother smilingly responds, "No, honey, you get to be a grown-up gradually. Before you're a grown-up person you have to learn many things, and one of those things is starting now. The other things come one by one, for instance, first you have to learn how to be a teenager. You know, you're just starting to be a teenager."

"Oh yeah, that's right. I have to learn a lot of things! Are the boys going to make fun of me now, mom?"

Her mother looks at her and smiles, "How will they know, unless you tell them?"

"They know, mom. They know when you get excused from gym, that's how they know."

"Oh, I see. And what if you don't get excused from gym?"

"Oh, ma, all the girls get excused from gym."

"Well, then, it sounds like you get excused from gym with a whole lot of other girls, so nobody's going to single you out."

"But what if I don't do it the same time as the other girls, mom?"

"And what if you don't get excused from gym?"

"Oh ... well, I have to think about that."

[158]

"OK, think about that . . . there are lots of ways to skin a cat. So you just figure out which one you like best."

"OK, OK, mom, OK. Say, mom, where did you put all those things you bought me? Remember you said you'd buy me those things. I bet you forgot. Did you forget mom, did you, did you forget?"

"No darling, I didn't forget. Go upstairs, and look in the linen closet in your bathroom. There in the back of the top shelf, you'll find a box, and there they are."

"Oh mom, I love you." And she throws her arms around her mother's neck whispering, "Now, do I have to be careful, and now do I have to not do certain things?"

"No, darling, you can do anything you want to do. I think it might be uncomfortable to go swimming wearing a pad, so you can see what you want to do about that. But you don't necessarily have to swim for those three days or so."

"Is that what I'll have, mom, three days?"

"I don't know, honey, sometimes your generation seems to have a shorter time, and maybe a heavier flow than we did. But I'm not sure. Women differ. So you will find out. Some have it for five days, some longer. And some have heavy flow for only one or two days, and are over it in three. It just depends."

"Oh, I see. Well, then, it will be sort of interesting to find out what I do."

"Yes, honey, it will."

"But why do I feel so teary, mom?"

"Perhaps because this is a first time, and you don't really know what to expect, do you?"

"Nope, that's true, mom, I don't know, I really don't."

"So it should be interesting for you, darling. You pay attention now to all the changes, and how you feel, and how it differs from how you feel when you're not having your period. So you can learn about yourself. Wouldn't that be fun?"

"Yeah, I guess so. Why do I feel . . . I should . . . I should be happy. I'm among the last of them, my friends, to get my period. And now, I'll be just like them and I should feel good, but I'm crying."

Her mother rocks her for a few moments, and strokes her hair. Then holding her gently, says, "Sometimes it seems that when we get our period and often for a day or two before, and sometimes a day or two after, our hormonal system makes a big adjustment, and our feelings are not our ordinary feelings because of that. Sometimes our feelings slide off center and are a little off kilter."

[159]

Her daughter looks intently at her, wide-eyed, fascinated. "So then are my hormones working, mom?"

Her mother laughs in spite of herself and says, "Yes, thank goodness, they are."

Her daughter smiles through her tears, and has to laugh a little too. "Well, you know, mom, it is sort of messy. It was kind of embarrassing."

Her mother nods, "Yes, you're not used to this, and you still are very unsure of yourself, but you'll get the knack of it, and in a few months' time, you really will take it as a matter of course. Besides, you always can have an extra supply in your locker at school, honey. Just keep it in a little box there, so that if this should happen in school again, there you'll be with everything you need."

"Oh mom, you're so comforting, and I'm so glad you're my mom."

Her mother smiles, holds her, rocks her back and forth a little, and says, "Actually it's an occasion to celebrate."

"Why is it to celebrate, mom?"

Her mother replies slowly, "It's to celebrate because today you have graduated into being a young woman instead of a child, and after today it's possible . . . although I hope you'll wait . . . it's possible for you to have a baby."

"Really, mom?"

"Well, of course. You see the supply of blood that you became aware of today has been stored up in your body for a very good reason."

"Oh I know mom, I know. It's for the ovum."

"That's right, my darling. But when the ovum hasn't been fertilized, then there isn't any need for the stored blood anymore."

"I know, mom, they told me about that in school."

"So you see, this is a very momentous occasion, and someday you will have a fertilized ovum, I hope, and it will fasten itself to the wall of your uterus, and you will have a wonderful supply of clean, healthy blood to nourish the new life that you'll be carrying."

"Oh, you make it sound so nice, mom. All the girls talk about the blood being dirty."

"Well, it isn't. It's the very best blood for the new life, darling, and it isn't dirty at all, and there is nothing about it that is anything but a cause for celebration. Do you know that in many places in the world, there are ceremonies to celebrate this? And there have been throughout the ages."

"Oh, wow, can we celebrate, mom?"

"Yes, indeed we can, darling. How would you like to celebrate?"

"Ooch, I don't know . . . I think I'd like to do some grown-up thing."

"And what might that be, darling?"

"Let me think, let me think. Could we go shopping?"

Her mother laughs, "It's a little late to go shopping today, but we could go shopping next Saturday if you like."

"I want to buy something grown-up to wear, mom."

"That's an excellent idea. Have you got something in mind?"

Her daughter hesitates, and then, "Not really, but . . . I don't know . . . maybe earrings."

Her mother laughs and says, "OK, we'll go shopping for earrings next Saturday. Will you want your ears pierced?"

"Oh, mom! . . . Does it hurt?"

"Oh, it didn't exactly hurt. It stung a little when I had mine done, but it didn't hurt that much. Would you like that?"

"Oh yes. You never would let me do it before, and now that I have my period, I've grown up enough."

Her mother laughs and hugs her, "That's right."

"How will I know when it's time to have a fertilized egg, mom?"

"Well, honey, I'm sure they told you in class that the best thing is to fertilize the egg with a young man you care very, very much about, that you care enough about to marry, so that you can provide a home for the new life. And so that the two of you can parent it, because a baby does best with two parents, you know. A baby really needs a mother and a father."

Her daughter looks at her wide-eyed.

"I know you know how eggs get fertilized. Isn't that right?"

"Yes, they told me in class."

"But what they might not have told you, darling, is that the very best way of all is when you plan, and when you both want to be parents. You marry because you love each other very much, and then you want to have a baby because that will be the most important union the two of you can have. A kind of confirmation that you are partners for life."

"Oh, mom, that is lovely. That is beautiful. But what if I never find someone whom I love that much? What if I never get married, mommy? Or what if after we get married something should happen . . . ?"

Her mother looks at her and says, "Like what?"

"Like figuring we made a mistake. And that we need to get a divorce. And we already have a baby. I know that happened to Mary

[161]

Lou's folks, and it also happened to Fran's. And I wonder what then, mom?"

"Well, those are sad things. And sometimes they do happen. That's why we need to be very thoughtful about the person we decide to be partners with. Before we get married we need to be pretty sure that is the person with whom we want to spend the rest of our lives."

"And what if it never happens to me, mom?"

Her mother smiles and looks at her fondly, and answers, "I think the chances are very good that it will happen to you."

"Say mom, think I ought to tell Mary and Jane?"

"That's up to you. Do they have their period?"

"Mary does, but Jane doesn't. If she has, she hasn't told me. That would be just like Jane not to say anything."

"Well, is it just like you not to say anything?"

"Um . . . maybe I'll say something first to Mary. Yeah, that would be fun, mom. I think I'll go over to Mary's and tell her. Oh boy, oh boy, that's great! OK, mom, I think I'll run on then. I'll just have time before supper . . . I'm gonna run down and see Mary."

And that's the end of the story.

Mama, Am I Pretty?

This is a story about a young girl in her very early teens. She looks quite familiar to you. She is talking with her mother, who also looks familiar to you. They are sitting in a pleasant room that looks like a sitting room or a study. They are seated at a card table, the mother on one side and her daughter at right angles, very close. Daughter is leaning her chin on her fist propping up her head, but looking down at the table and talking very earnestly.

She is saying, "Mama, am I pretty?"

Her mother looks at her intently, smiles and says, "I think you are very pretty."

"Well, I'm wondering if I'm very pretty because some of my friends . . . especially Joy, is very, very pretty. She has this curly blonde hair. You know, mom?"

Her mother replies, "Yes, I know your friend Joy. She is very pretty."

"Well, you know, mom, a couple of the boys always seem to hang around wherever Joy is. And what they do is kid around with each other, not with Joy, but like they're, I don't know, mom, like they're kinda showing off for Joy. Joy pretends not to notice but later on she comes back and giggles about it. And she talks about how Joe calls her up at night and wants to hang on the phone with nothing at all to say, just 'uhs' and 'ahs' and 'whatchadoing' and 'see ya', and I don't know what all. Then as soon as he's off the line, Bill is on the line saying, 'Boy, do you have a busy phone.' And he's 'uhing' and 'ahing' without too much to say either. So I figured that Joy is so pretty the boys are paying a lot of attention to her. But you know, mom, no boy seems to notice me at all except that yucky old Paul. And who would want HIM to pay attention?"

Her mother laughs and says, "I think Paul's pretty cute."

"Oh, mom, he's really square."

"Oh? What is square about him? What is it you find square?"

"He just isn't really with it, mom, you know. The other guys seem . . . I don't know. He just seems dull to me, like he doesn't have much going for him. And anyway, I don't like how he dresses."

"Oh? How does he dress?"

"I know this sounds just awful, mom, but he doesn't wear the right kind of jeans and his hair is too long."

"Wow," exclaims her mother, "that is a long list of things wrong with him, I can see that. Are clothes and haircuts really that important?"

Her daughter looks at her and says, "Well, you know, mom, I wouldn't admit this to anybody except you or, maybe, I don't know, but maybe dad, but yeah, with the kids that's important."

Her mother looks at her and asks, "Are those things important to you?"

"Gee, I can hear that it sounds kinda yucky, but yep, I think right now that it's important to me. I know it's important to me that I wear the right kind of jeans and shoes and everything."

"Oh? How do you decide what are the right things?"

"You know, mom, it's what's 'in,' what's fashionable."

"Yes, I can understand that . . . and I guess before you get to know somebody you do kind of judge them by how they fit in. And I suppose it's very important right now that people fit in, right?"

"Yep, mom, it is."

"All right, I can understand that. But meanwhile, I know something very, very nice about Paul."

Her daughter looks at her skeptically and says, "Yeah?"

"Yes. He likes you. And I like that about him."

"Oh, yep, yep, just so long as he doesn't hang around so much that the other guys will be turned off of me."

Her mother smiles. "The others are going to pay attention to you, honey. Just give them a little time. You have to remember that the boys in your class are emotionally a year or so behind the girls. Did you know that? So those 13-year-old boys really seem young compared with the girls. Does it seem that way to you?"

Her daughter nods and looks at her with surprise.

"And that pretty well happens, honey, until you get to be, maybe

18, 19, or 20, and even then, often the 21-year-old man is a little young for a 20-year-old woman."

"Yeah, I can see that, mom. How much older than you is dad?"

Her mother smiles, "Well, actually, three years older."

"Oh, and would you say that's just right, mom?"

Her mother smilingly answers, "There is no 'just right.' But when you get to that stage, it's not really important what kind of jeans he wears. That can always be changed. But there are other things in a person that are not so easily changed. So at that time it's very important that you like those harder-to-change things."

Her daughter looks pensive, and then asks, "When will boys begin to pay attention to me, mom?"

"I would say very soon, darling, because you have started to pay attention to them."

And that's the end of the scene.

Adolescence

Mother-Daughter Talk

This is a story about a young girl. She looks to be a very young girl on the threshold of puberty. She looks familiar to you. She is talking with her mother. They are sitting at a table, I believe it's in the kitchen. The young girl has a glass of milk in front of her. Her mother is drinking out of a cup. It looks as though it might be coffee or tea. And they are having a little chat. They're laughing. It's casual and very pleasant.

But then a little frown comes over the young girl's face as she looks down into her glass of milk. She studies it very carefully as if trying to figure something out. Her mother's attention is caught. She tilts her head a little, and raises her eyebrows slightly as she watches her daughter. She waits, very still, very attentive. Her daughter clears her throat and says, "Mom," and her mom says, "Um hm?" And her daughter says, "Um, I've been thinking," and she looks up at her mother, catches her eye, and then looks quickly down again into her milk.

"I've been thinking about how I want to ask some questions, but, you know, I go to these classes at school. They have these sex education classes, mom."

And her mom says gently, "Yes, yes, I know."

"But I don't like to ask questions there, and anyway they make it into . . . I don't know, they talk about stuff and it sounds like they read it out of a book, and I am too embarrassed to ask questions. None of the other kids ask questions either. Everybody just sits there. Sometimes they giggle, and sometimes they look at each other, and sometimes we just sit. And anyway, I would never ask questions in front of the boys. That would be humiliating!"

Her mother smiles and says, "Well, I can certainly understand how you feel. So what questions do you want to ask?"

"Well you know, mom, I know where babies come from and all that. They teach us that. And I also know how a woman gets the egg fertilized, OK? And I understand what the boy, I mean the man does, sort of. But you know, mom, it seems so gross."

Her mother looks at her seriously, as she responds, "Well, I do understand what you mean."

"Do you mom?"

"Yes, but maybe they forgot to tell you that when you love somebody very much, then being very affectionate and being very close to them can culminate in the sex act . . . which is wonderful when it's with someone you love very much. . . . And it's really not much if you don't."

"Oh, is that how it is, mom?"

"You bet. That's why, when you're very young, as you are, and even for some years to come, honey, it's wise for you not to experiment with sex, because you are not old enough. You haven't had enough experience with different boys or young men to choose someone that you would truly love. So it probably would not be a good experience. And possibly it could be so disappointing that it just might be hurtful to you."

"Oh, I can understand that, mom, I can understand that! And, anyway, yuck, I don't like any of the boys in our class They are really awful."

Her mother smilingly replies, "Well, you know, at your age young girls mature and develop a year or so ahead of the boys their same age. Did you know that?"

"Well, I know they're awfully short, mom, and they seem silly to me. The girls seem much more grown up although some of them are pretty silly, too, I guess."

Her mother smiles as she responds, "Well, in a little while you'll be meeting older boys, and when they are a little older than you, they'll be just right for you."

"Oh, mom, I don't really . . . I don't know, I don't really want to meet anybody yet. I'm not ready! I really don't want to!"

"Well, I can understand that, honey. Is there anything else you want to ask?"

"Um-m, I guess I really want to ask about babies."

"What about babies?"

"Well, I know where they come from, like I told you, but it just

[170]

seems to me impossible that a baby could grow that big inside you. Doesn't it hurt?"

"No, actually not. I guess you know it takes nine months for a baby to develop."

"Yeah, yeah, I know that."

"And actually for the first four months, sometimes even five months, it's usually a very comfortable feeling. I remember that I felt very pleased, pleased with myself, and my body felt very good. They say that when a woman is pregnant all of her hormones and all of her organs and everything in her body and even in her mind become harmonious. That she really feels better at that time than at any other time in her life. Many women have said that."

Her daughter is sitting there looking at her with wide-open eyes, drinking in every word.

"Then, later, when you get bigger and the baby gets heavier, it is a little awkward. Sometimes it's awkward to walk. You may have noticed pregnant women, they seem to be leaning backward as if to balance the load better. They walk sort of with a little waddle, and sometimes at night it's a little uncomfortable in bed. You can't sleep on your tummy, you know."

"Oh, gosh, I always sleep on my tummy. I can't imagine what I'll do."

"You will be so pleased that you're going to have a little baby that you'll easily learn to sleep on your side, darling, or on your back."

"Oh, well, I don't know," the young girl murmurs, and then, "Mom, gosh, what if there's something wrong with the baby?"

"Oh, all pregnant women have thoughts about that. That is something that we all are a little afraid of. But if you look around you at the world . . . or just look around your school room. How many kids are there in your room?"

"We have 23, mom."

"Well, there are 23 kids there and once they were all infants. They all got born just the same way as I'm describing it, and they're all fine. So how do you think that averages out?"

Her daughter laughs in spite of herself. "Well, mom, I guess the majority of babies are OK."

"That's exactly right. And you're a fine healthy young woman, and you will probably marry a healthy young man, and you will have a healthy baby."

Her daughter sighs a small sigh of relief and says, "Oh gee, mom, you're wonderful! You really know just what to say to me."

[171]

Her mother reaches over to pat her daughter's hand and says, "You're pretty wonderful yourself. You're a very wise child, and I always pay attention to what you say because I can use your good sense."

Her daughter smiles and adds, "But mom, there's one more thing." "OK, what is it?"

"I heard that when the baby starts to come the pain is really terrible. It's just the worst pain you ever could imagine to have in your whole life."

Her mother looks at her as she thoughtfully replies, "Do you know that nowadays, when you're going to have a baby, they teach you how?"

"What do you mean, mom?"

"Well, you have lessons on how to breathe, and what to do, and the position to take. All of which makes it less painful and helps the baby get born. Then if it gets too bad at any time, and usually toward the end sometimes it can be pretty painful, they give you some medication. Then the baby comes out. You open your eyes, and you hear that wonderful sound! It's the most wonderful, beautiful sound in the whole world! It's your baby yelling at the top of its lungs!"

Her young daughter bursts into laughter and exclaims, "You think that's a wonderful sound, mom?"

"Just you wait, and you'll know what I mean. And now I'm going to tell you something very interesting. And it isn't just my own experience, but almost every woman that I've talked with about this tells me she had the same experience. You cannot remember the pain! You know you had it but you just don't remember. It goes out of your head completely, and when they put that little bundle in your arms, and you unwrap it to see if it has all its fingers, and all its toes, and it's truly a girl, or a boy, whatever gender they told you it is . . . you will know a joy that can only be equaled by the joy you feel when the baby's father joins you and you present his baby to him. It is a wonderful, wonderful moment that no woman ever forgets."

"Gee, mom, you make it sound beautiful."

"Well, I guess I think it is beautiful."

"OK, I just wanted to know about that. And there are some other things I wonder about, but right now I really have to go. I promised Betsy that I'd go shopping with her. She wants to buy a skirt, and I was going to help her pick it out."

Her mother asks, looking at her, "Would you like a new skirt, too?

[172]

Do you need one?" Her daughter, giggling, replies, "Well, you know mom, I don't need one, but I can always use one."

Her mother smiles at her, "Well, go ahead, don't be extravagant, but go ahead."

"Oh, mom, you are super, oh you really are super!" She flings her arms around her mother's neck and is gone in an instant.

And that is the end of the episode.

Nascent Courtship

This is a story about four young girls talking together. They are in a girl's bedroom with the door shut.

"Don't you dare tell anybody!"

"Oh no, we would not do that, honestly we wouldn't do that!"

And they start whispering again to each other, gossiping.

"Do you know about Alyssa? Well, Alyssa and Mack, they meet after school almost every day and then they go out there, you know, in the woods, and I heard . . . "

"What, what did you hear?"

Then they whisper, whisper, whisper, whisper, whisper.

"Oh, come on," one young girl protests, "I don't!"

"Oh, you think so?"

And another speaks, "Well I don't know, I don't know . . . oh gee, oh wow, poor Alyssa."

"You don't have to feel sorry for Alyssa! Alyssa's the one always calling him up, and Alyssa's the one who waits around. Alyssa is the one who gets things going, I think."

"Oh, well, I don't know . . . "

And then they whisper some more and then, "Oh no, I would never do that! Oh no, no, no, I wouldn't like to do that! No! And anyway, who wants to do that with those dirty old boys?"

"Well, I don't know," Cindy blurts out, "I don't want to do THAT, of course, but I wouldn't mind if Tommy waited for me after school . . . and maybe we could walk home together and get to know each other a little better."

"What's to know? You've known Tommy since he was five years old in kindergarten."

"Well, you know, it's different now."

"Oh," exclaims another girl in disgust. "That's it! There goes Cindy."

And Cindy protests, "Oh come on! Don't be silly. That's not so, that's just not so!"

"Well, then, what is all this talk about how you would like to walk home with Tommy?"

"Well, I just think it would be nice to get to know a boy a little better."

"Well, girls, I guess we're going to walk home in a threesome now."

"Don't be silly, he has never even waited for me! He has no idea that I want him to wait!"

"You want us to tell him?"

"No! No! Don't you dare, don't you dare! Promise that you won't."

"OK, OK, But how do you expect him to ask you if he never knows?"

"I don't know. Well, I'm just hoping that maybe sometime, just by accident, we could maybe meet right after school and be going the same way or something."

"Ahhh, you could wait until you're a gray-haired old lady before that dumb old Tommy ever notices anything."

"Oh, I don't think you have to put him down like that! I really don't think you ought to put him down like that! I think he's kinda nice."

"So we heard, so we heard."

But then another small voice pipes up, 'Well, I think I understand. It's not that I really want to do what Alyssa does . . . but you know Hal?"

"Yes," a little chorus of yesses.

"Well, Hal asked if I ever go to the store after school, and I said, 'Sure.' Then he asked if maybe I would like to meet him there sometime and we could get a soda."

"Oh, for heaven's sake," the other two exclaim in unison, disgusted. "Will you do it?"

"Well, maybe. I don't know, it might be fun. Don't you think it might be fun?"

"Uh oh, there goes another one!" groan the two, who can't understand at all how their friends could be interested in those nasty boys. They just sit there, glumly, looking at their friends and picking at the nap on the carpet.

Finally Cindy looks up brightly and says, "Hey, you guys, how about going down to the kitchen and getting a soda? Then we could go on out and ride our bikes. How about that?"

"Good idea! Enough of this silly talk. We need some fresh air."

And off they go.

That's the end of this episode.

First Date

This story is about a young adolescent girl. She is sprawled on the floor with her head resting against the side of her bed. In her lap is a telephone and she holds the receiver between her shoulder, the mattress and her ear. She's set for a very long leisurely conversation with one of her girlfriends. There are lots of giggles and "Oh, you don't mean it! . . . No kidding!"

Then she starts to talk. "Well, did you see him today?" Obviously she's talking about a boyfriend, giggling a lot and saying, "Oh, I don't know, he's kinda cute but . . . " and then listening, then nodding, then grinning, and then saying, "Oh yeah, yeah, he is. Yes, he is. No, I didn't notice that one. Oh, is that so, well, isn't that . . . what do you know . . . " The conversation continues, talking and comparing notes about boys in the class.

Then she begins talking about an upcoming party. They're going to have a big party at school. It's going to be a Halloween party. A long discussion starts. "What are you going to wear? . . . Well, I don't know. . . . What are you going as? . . . Well, I've been thinking about it . . . I'm really sick of witches and ghosts and stuff like that. I'd really like to go as something different but I don't know what." There follows a long conversation about what to wear.

There's a light tap on the door and mother puts her head in around the door, "May I come in?"

The young girl says into the phone, "Hey, listen, I'll call you back . . . yep, yep, I'll call you back in a little while. OK. Bye." She hangs up.

Mom comes in the room, sits down and says, "I thought I'd come in and have a little visit tonight. Earlier today you said that there were some things you were wondering about and I thought maybe you would like to talk about it?"

The young girl nods, "Yep." She stays sprawled out on the floor, so mother pulls up a low stool and sits down near her.

"Well go ahead . . . shoot."

The young girl looks up at the ceiling and down at her hands and then around the room and says, "Well, uh, some of the kids are dating."

Her mother smiles and says, "Yes?"

"Well, uh, there's this boy, Johnny, at school and, you know, he wants me to go to the Halloween party with him and I've never gone to any party with a boy. I just went with, uh, my friends, you know. He wants to take me to the party. He says he wants a date, and I feel funny about that, mom."

"Well, what is it that feels funny to you? Are your other friends going with boys? Are they having a date?"

"Well, some of them, most of them not, mom, but some of them."

"Well, what do you think about maybe joining forces with some of those who are going with boys so you aren't just going as couples but maybe four or six together."

"Well, I don't know, I don't know. . . . I guess I could ask the girls."

"Well sure, why not? Although I don't see anything wrong with going to the party with just Johnny if you enjoy his company . . . and you know you can have fun with the others as well. You don't have to talk and dance just with Johnny exclusively, do you?"

"Well I don't know what you do, mom. That's what I'm talking about, I just don't know what you do. And I don't want to just talk to him and dance only with him. I like him OK but you know, I just . . . well, I guess I want to tell you something that happened, mom. The other day I was walking down the street on the way to school and I hear these footsteps running and there he is. He's walking with me."

"Who? Johnny?"

"Yes. And he says, 'How about meeting me after school? Uh . . . uh, maybe we could talk.' And I say, 'Well, OK, if, uh . . . where do you want to meet?' He said, 'I'll be waiting for you out there at the entrance.' And sure enough there he was when I came out, mom, and I felt very funny. I had a funny feeling in the pit of my stomach. I don't know why that was."

"Well, were you feeling a little anxious because you didn't know what he wanted, and that this was kind of different behavior?"

"Well, I don't know, mom, I just had this funny feeling and I didn't like it. I really don't like to feel like that, mom. Is there something wrong with me?"

Her mother answers with a smile, "Not at all, honey. All it means is that you are growing up, and you're growing up so fast that it makes you feel a little queasy. I guess that must be it. And also I think you don't know what to expect, so maybe that's the reason. What do you think?"

"Well, mom, maybe, maybe, I don't know. Well, anyway, let me tell you what he said. He wanted to go over and sit under a tree. So we sat down next to each other under a tree and first thing I know he had his arm around my shoulder. I edged away and shrugged my shoulders and he said, 'What's the matter?' and I said, 'Well, I don't know. I'm uncomfortable. I don't want you to put your arm around my shoulders.' Then he said, 'Oh, it's like that is it? I was going to ask you to be my girl.' And I said, 'What do you mean . . . *be my girl* . . . ?' He said, 'Well I wanted to ask you to go steady with me. Uh . . . uh . . . I like you a lot and I would just like you to be my girl.' 'I don't want to be your girl,' I said. And mom, he looked so sad, he looked so down, and I felt mean but I don't know what that means, 'be his girl'."

"I see . . . well, sometimes boys and girls single each other out, and they both like each other at that time more than they like other boys or girls. Then what they want is to have a friendship that is very special and very concentrated."

"Well, I don't know if I like him that much, mom. I feel funny. I don't want him putting his arm around me. And yet, I'm not sure, mom. I'm not sure, mom."

"Well, you know, when you are the age you are . . . some girls a little older, some a little younger . . . uh, you begin making choices among people. You begin getting ready for courtship, and way, way, way down the line, prepare for the special relationship that we call marriage. And in order to get ready for that, honey, we have to have experiences with many young men, some as friends and some as closer than friends. And you need to think about that, because without experience how will you know how to choose the special one you're going to marry?"

"Well, mom, you know some girls, some girls, uh, do things I don't want to do.'

"I see. Well, you know darling, your body is your own to decide about, yourself, and no one else may decide that for you. But I will tell you this. I really believe that it's better to be very choosy and better to go very, very slowly. And not to engage in real sexual activity until you have had a lot of friendships with a lot of different boys and girls. Only then can you begin to really decide with what sort of person you might want to spend the rest of your life. And you are still too young to decide that yet, because you haven't known enough different people. Now I know that young kids experiment, and they kiss, and they touch, and if you really truly want to do that and are sure that you're in charge of what happens next, and sure that you will go slowly and thoughtfully, I think that's part of growing up."

"Well, mom, some kids, uh uh . . . do it."

Her mother looks at her, and then pauses for a long moment, before saying, "I think that's too bad, because real sexual intercourse needs to proceed from love, and love needs to grow from friendship, only then can it be beautiful. Otherwise it just becomes mechanical and very shallow. So I hope that you will wait until you are much more experienced before you will even consider having sex on that level with Johnny or any other young man who might try to persuade you. It is true that young boys, young men, have a physical urgency that is very different from what most young women feel. And under the pressure of that urgency, they often rush their lives and rush their relationships. Many of them regret it afterwards . . . really feel ashamed and embarrassed. And often, in a strange way, they feel differently about the young girl than they did before. It's not that they care less for her, but that they feel ashamed and scared. So I hope you will be very thoughtful, my darling."

After a pause, mother continues, "I'm very glad that you came and asked me about it, because I know how hard it is for a young person, just beginning to take her first steps into adulthood, to tell her mom or her dad about this kind of thing. I just want you to know, darling, that I think that you are a very intelligent and very wise young person. I feel confident that you will take care of yourself, and be thoughtful of yourself, and will ask yourself what your goals really are, and what you really do enjoy. You know we still have rules in our house. They're not many, but there are rules, and you know that we all, living together in our house, observe these rules, and so I trust that you will continue to do so. At the same time I am aware that you must take your steps out into your own world, getting ready to be a grown-up."

Her daughter throws her arms around her mother's neck, exclaiming, "Oh mom, you are the greatest!"

Her mother hugs her and that is the end of this story.

First
Sexual Encounter

This episode is about a young adolescent boy, perhaps 13 or 14 years old. He looks very familiar to you. He's talking to his dad, who also looks familiar to you. They are sitting in a room that seems to be a study or home office. They sit opposite each other, dad lounging back in an armchair, and son sitting on the ottoman with his elbows on his knees, leaning forward and gazing very earnestly at his father.

He's saying, "Gee dad, I'm having a hard time talking about this. I feel very embarrassed, and I think I'm a little bit scared."

"What are you scared of, son?"

The young boy replies, "Well, I think maybe you're going to take a very . . . mmm . . . well, you're not going to be very pleased with what I'm going to tell you, dad."

With raised eyebrows his father asks, "Well, how do you know?"

"I really don't know, dad. But we never have talked about this, and I don't feel real good about it myself, to tell you the truth."

"OK, son. Do you think you might feel better if you did talk about it?"

"Yeah, yeah, I guess so, dad. . . . Well, you see it's like this: There's this young girl. Well, she's not exactly a girl. She's a lot older than I am, dad."

His father raises his eyebrows again.

"Yeah, dad, I guess she must be 17 or 18, something like that. I don't know for sure. She didn't tell me, but she looks pretty old."

"Oh."

"Yeah, dad, well there's this . . . I stop in at this food place sometimes on my way home from school, you know, one of these places with a counter. She waits on the counter, and I would stop in and

[181]

have a soda or something, you know, and we'd get to talking. I thought she was pretty nice. She's kinda nice, and very friendly, and she always seemed so glad to see me, and we would joke around. We would kid around, and joke around, and well, Saturday, dad, she asked me what I was doing that evening and I just shrugged and said, 'Oh, I don't know, just foolin' around.' She said, 'I'm off at nine o'clock. You wanna come by and maybe we could do something?'

"I just looked at her. I was real surprised, dad, because she's so old, but I thought maybe I look older than I am to her. So I wasn't gonna let on. She'd just think I'm silly, you know, just a kid, and I didn't want her to think that. Anyway, I, well, to tell you the truth, I was very curious.

"So I showed up about . . . well, I went over there at nine and I hung around outside. I kinda got cold feet but I thought, 'Oh well, what the heck,' and I went in, and there she was sitting at one of the tables. She got up when she saw me and ran over to where I was, and said, 'Come on, let's go.' I didn't know where she wanted to go, but I said, 'OK.' So there she was. She looked kinda cute. She had on a pretty dress that had a kinda ruffle around the neck, very cute and pretty. And she has pretty hair. It's kinda reddish hair, curly, and she had on kinda a lot of make-up, but I figured that was because she's kinda old and you know. . . .

"Down there on Spruce Street there's that little park, and there's some buildings in that little park. You know the sort of place where they keep all the tools and stuff, and uh, she whispered at me, 'I know a place that we can go.' I said, 'Uh, a place? What kinda place?' She stood back and looked at me. Then she gave me a little shove, and she said, 'Oh, you know.' And so I didn't want to let on that I didn't know, so I said, 'Oh, yeah, yeah, sure.' So we went over there where, back in the shadows, there's one of these little buildings. She pushed the door open. I looked in, and God, I don't know, it looked kinda, kinda scary to me in there, you know. I didn't know what was in there, but she said, 'Come on, hurry up.' And so I went in with her and she pulled the door closed and she said, 'We're OK here. Nobody will come here. They don't use this place except in the mornings when they get their stuff, and I know it's OK.' I just looked at her like a dummy and I said, 'OK?' She said, 'Yes, OK. It's OK in here. Just come on over here.'

"There in the corner, a couple of old blankets were folded up. She plopped herself down on them, dad, and then she held out her arms, and so I sat down. I didn't know exactly what to do, so she grabs me and she kisses me, and she really kisses me. You know dad, how I mean, she kisses, I mean, I never kissed anybody like that before. I don't know if I even liked it, dad, but I didn't want to act like a dumb kid. And then in a way I did like it, in a funny way. I felt scared and at the same time I was kinda disgusted. I don't know how to tell you . . . but she unzipped my pants, dad, and she started, you know, and, and God, I didn't know what to do, but I did get kinda excited. And before I knew it, I was doing it."

His father looks at him and asks, "Doing it?"

"Well, yeah, you know, I was screwing her, dad."

"Oh, I see, son."

"And when it was over I got up and I straightened out my clothes, and she kinda straightened out her clothes, and she said, 'You got any money on you?' I was really surprised, but I said, 'Gee, yeah, I gotta dollar and I guess some change. Why?' She said, 'Well, I'm kinda broke and I need a little money, so I thought maybe you'd lend it to me.' So I gave her the dollar and sixteen cents. That was all the rest of my allowance. And I thought, 'Gee, this is funny, this is real funny, and I'm not sure I like this at all.' And then she stood up and put her arms around me, and said, 'How about a little goodnight kiss, sweetheart?' So I said, 'OK,' but I didn't really want to kiss her, dad. And I couldn't wait to leave. When we got outside I said, 'Well, so long, I'll be seeing you.' Then I all but ran home and when I got here I got in the shower. Gee, I felt rotten, I really felt rotten."

His dad nods, "Yes, son, I see that you did. I'm real sorry that your first experience was like that, because I want to tell you something. We'll talk about this again, but what I want to tell you is that what you experienced was not lovemaking. What you experienced was sex without love, and I believe that is always disappointing. And what you experienced you were not ready for. You didn't really know what was involved. Shall we talk about this some more another time?"

His son replies hesitantly, "Yeah, dad, I guess I would like to."

Then his father adds, "The only thing I want to say before we stop for now, is that I'm glad that you told me, because I think that, even though it was hard for you to do, it is even harder for you just to keep it all inside yourself and not talk about it with someone that you can trust. And I want you to know I feel very proud that you trusted me. OK, son?"

His son is shyly smiling at him and replies, "Gee, you really are something else again, dad. Thanks."

And that's the end of the episode.

[183]

Father and Son Discuss Courtship

The scene opens with a father sitting in his armchair with his young son across from him on the ottoman, leaning his face on his fists watching his father intently, as he asks him, "Well, dad, how do I find somebody, uh, you know, somebody, a girl, and know that I really am in love, and that she's the right one, and you know, how do I go about it? You know, dad, I feel very . . . well . . . scared."

His dad smiles at him and says, "Well, son, I surely understand that because it's very natural to feel quite unsure of yourself and a little afraid, perhaps, that you aren't going to be able to do the right thing or say the right thing . . . or even be able to tell, perhaps, if it's someone you really could care for. Is that it?"

"Yeah, that's about it, dad. You know, I talk to the fellas. As a matter of fact, that's about all we talk about now. And some of them talk about how they have a line, and how the girls react to them, and how they make time with them, dad."

And dad replies, "Yeah, I know exactly what you mean. That's male talk and has been, I suspect, since the beginning of time. But really it's just a way for them to try on for size all their courtship maneuvers. You've seen *National Geographic* illustrations, and you've seen videos about the courtship of birds, for example, how the male peacock spreads his tail feathers. The males are gorgeous and impressive, and their little brown hens watch, obviously overwhelmed with admiration, as they strut around and wave their fans of gorgeous feathers in the air. And you've seen some birds do a kind of dance, and fight other birds. This maneuvering is all a part of courtship, son."

The boy looks at him, nods, and says, "Yep, yeah, I guess so dad," and then he laughs, as he says, "Anyway, you make it sound so funny."

His dad smiles at him, "Well, in many ways it is a little humorous, perhaps, and incidentally that is a very important point. We need to remember that courting, and all of the maneuvers that lead to relationships are playful. It isn't, doesn't have to be, deadly serious. The best courting is having fun and being playful, having a good time, not taking yourself too seriously. Heavy-heavy really isn't as productive as approaching all of these relationships as a way to have pleasure and fun."

"Well, dad, that's really interesting to me, because the guys, when they talk about it, they sound like they try to be very earnest and very sincere. And that's their line. Other ones try to be indifferent and kinda strutting around like, well, actually like peacocks, dad."

His dad laughs as he says, "I know. But if you will keep it in mind that when you see a young woman whom you find attractive, and most of all, whom you like, then you can approach her from the point of view of 'Let's play together. Let's have fun together.' And that's really what dating should be. If you will take it step by step, son, then you can begin your relationship first on the basis of liking each other, and being friends. Of course, there's always this undercurrent of being sexually attracted as well. But that doesn't have to be played up as the point of the whole thing at the beginning of a relationship. It's much better to get to know each other and to see if you really like her and she really likes you. I think it's extremely important that neither of you acts so hastily or so prematurely that you scare each other."

"Well, dad, I don't have to wait or be careful. I'm already scared, I'm scared before I start."

His dad chuckles and says, "Yeah, yeah, I know, son, but all the same, you can remember that she's scared, too. So there you are, two scared kids. And you know that you are. Remember how you were with your little puppy. When you first got your little puppy she was scared, remember. She probably was missing her mama, and was scared about all the strange people, and the new strange place. Remember, she even piddled because she was so scared when you first brought her in."

His son chuckles and says, "Yeah, I remember."

Then his dad asks him, "Do you remember how you made friends with her? You were gentle and you stroked her a little. Now I'm not saying that you would physically stroke a young lady whom you first met. But you can be gentle and stroke in other ways . . . smiling, small

[185]

talk, movies, rides, walks in the park perhaps, talks on the park bench, that kind of thing. You know what I mean."

"Gee, dad, that really sounds pretty relaxed."

"That's exactly the whole idea. Make friends with a young woman who attracts you the way you would make friends with a young man. Be pleasant, be warm, be friendly in the same way, and you will find that, without realizing it, both of you will stop being scared. And then, if you really have something worth developing between the two of you, after a while you both will, probably without even consciously thinking about it, move into the next stage of your courtship. You will continue to be gentle, take it easy, not rush things, allow her to react and to initiate, as well as you. And then, son, it might develop into a sexual relationship . . . and mind you, I'm not telling you that I consider you ready for a sexual relationship, as yet. Because from what you have told me I suspect that you need more experience with quite a few different young ladies until you find someone who would really be suitable for you."

"Well, dad, I could get to be 30 years old."

His father hoots with laughter, "No, I really don't think it will take that long."

His son laughs a little sheepishly, and his dad adds, "And then, should you move into the sexual phase, then it's very important that you know how to protect yourself and her."

"Oh, you mean, like birth control, dad?"

"Yes, but you know, son, birth control has taken on a whole different aspect in the last few years, and that is because of the danger now of incurable sexually transmitted diseases."

"Oh, gee, dad, I would never even take up with a girl who had, you know, was sexually diseased."

"Well, son, what I'm saying is that there are sexual diseases like herpes. Have you heard of herpes?"

"Oh sure, dad, as a matter of fact, I know somebody who has it."

His father continues, "Well, I guess we all know someone, son. All the more reason to be cautious. He didn't get it, your friend, because he thought there was any danger of getting it. He got it because he didn't consider that there possibly might be, OK?"

"Yeah, yeah, you're right, dad."

"Well then, there is the question of AIDS. This is a very serious, and so far, incurable sexually transmitted disease. So you must decide that you will not have sexual intercourse with anyone you don't know very, very well. And knowing very, very well would include being tested for AIDS and physically examined for other possible diseases as is now the custom before marriage. And before marriage, it would be wise for you, son, to always use a condom."

"Gosh dad, all the boys say that's just like, well, to put it in their words, 'like washing your feet with your socks on'."

His father laughs and says, "Well, that isn't quite an accurate description. Anyway, so far, it is the only safe way that we know. You need to read this pamphlet on AIDS and on herpes. It's up there sticking out of the bookcase. See it on the third shelf there near the end? I would like you to take that down and read it carefully. And if you have any questions, you know my door is always open."

"Gee, dad," said his son, "You're so, you're just such a neat dad."

His dad reaches his arms around his son's shoulders and hugs him tightly for an instant. Then he gives him a little shove as he says, "Well, I am very proud of the way that you are growing up. I can see that you are going to make a good life for yourself."

And that's the end of the episode.

First Love

This is a story about a mother and daughter. The mother is saying to her daughter, "That's a very interesting question you're asking me, honey. And I can understand a lot of the uncertainty that you must feel. I can remember when I was 14 and how uncertain I felt about boys, and now that you seem to be forming a friendship with Pete, I'm glad that you want to talk about it."

"Sure, mom. You know, I like Pete. He's really cool. You know, he's on the school team. He plays on the football team. He's on the first team, and he's good. And he is good looking, mom."

Her mother smiles with pleasure, and says, "I've seen him. I agree. He's a very fine looking young man."

"And I really like him, mom, you know. He's smart, too. He gets good grades, and he wants to come over and study here some time with me. Would that be OK?"

Her mother looks at her smiling, "Why sure, honey, that would be super. Are you in the same classes?"

"In two. We're in math and in history."

"Good, maybe you can help each other come exam time, ask each other questions, and things like that, I mean."

"Yeah, mom, that would be fun, wouldn't it?"

Her mother smiles, "Sure."

"Sometimes when I'm in the library, mom, he comes over and he sits next to me and we write notes back and forth."

Her mother laughs a little and says, "That sounds like a good game."

Her daughter tries to suppress a smile, looks down, and says, "He writes, ummmmm, 'I love you'."

Her mother looks at her, raises her eyebrows and says, "He does? And what do you write back?"

Her daughter looks down again, and says, "I don't. I just look at him and smile."

Her mother chuckles and says, "That is wise, honey."

Her daughter asks, "Why is that wise, mom?"

"Because it shows that you're not displeased but that you're not ready to return it in kind. Or does it mean something else?"

"Well, I don't know, I don't know really what to say. I don't know if I love him or not. How do you know if you love somebody, mom?"

"I'm not sure. But one thing I am sure of: when you do, you don't have to ask that question."

"Oh, oh, OK." Then she adds, "Mom, sometimes when we're coming home after being at someone's house, you know, and Pete walks me home at night, um . . . he kisses me at the door."

Her mother looks at her and asks, "Oh? And do you like that?"

Her daughter nods her head but avoids her eyes, and her mother says, "I guess that's all right. How do you feel about being that affectionate with a boy whom you really don't know that well?"

"Oh, but I do, mom, I know him very well. I see him every day."

"Yes, but you haven't really been doing things with Pete as your partner, have you?"

"Oh, sure, mom. Let's see, it's going to be 15 days tomorrow."

Her mother laughs out loud. Her daughter looks up and has to laugh, too. "I guess that isn't very long, is it mom?"

"No, it's not very long to get to really know somebody. I think that it's OK to kiss goodnight, but perhaps it would be a good idea to limit it to just a goodnight kiss until you and Pete get to know each other a good deal better. What do you think? You're still pretty young, you know."

"Oh come on, mom, most of the girls are dating at my age."

Her mother looks at her ruefully, and says, "I know, but I am not sure how wise it is to be pairing off when you have had so little experience with other boys, and still have no basis of experience for how to proceed."

"Well, mom, I don't have to proceed at all, I just keep on doing what we're doing."

"What do the other girls say about what's happening with them?"

"Some of them, you know, uh, one especially, I don't even want to say her name . . . she's pretty . . . I don't know . . . she's pretty wild."

"Why, what does she do, honey?"

[189]

"Well, first of all, mom, she smokes."

Her mother asks, "And have you tried smoking?"

"Yeah, I did once, but, mom, I didn't like it, I didn't like how it tasted and I didn't like how it smelled, and it did make me a little sick."

"Good, I'm glad, because that's something nobody needs to do."

"You know, this girl I'm telling you about, well, the boys really do hang around her."

"Oh, is that so? Is she that pretty, and is she that interesting, or what is it that they all like about her so much?"

"Well, mom," and her daughter half whispers, "the other girls say she puts out."

Her mother looks at her and says, "Puts out?"

"You know, mom, she meets them places like in the park, and they go back into the trees and bushes and they make out."

"Oh, do a lot of the girls in your class do that?"

"I don't think so, mom, but she does, and I'm wondering. I know that's not all right to do because all the other girls shake their heads and whisper about her. But the boys sure seem to like her."

Her mother nods, "Yes, that's true, the boys like her now but they won't like her very long. Other boys will come along while she's still young and pretty and wild. But in the long run I think she probably is doing herself great harm."

"How is that, mom?"

"First of all, if what you're saying is that she's having sex with these boys . . . Is that what you're saying, dear?"

"Yeah, mom, that's about the general idea," getting red in the face.

"Well," her mother responds, "In the first place, in these times, that's very, very dangerous. Not only is she risking getting pregnant, which really would be too bad because she's not ready to be a mother to a little baby. And certainly the boy . . . "

"Uh, it's not just one, mom . . . "

"Well, then whoever the boys are, they certainly aren't ready to be a father to a little baby. And that's a very sad thing to do, to bring a little baby into the world without a mother who is willing and able to mother it, or a father who is willing or able to father it. Don't you think?"

"Oh, yes, mom, oh, I would never want that to happen to me. That is horrible."

"Yes, I think that's pretty serious, yes indeed. And then there are other things. Even if she doesn't get pregnant, there's danger if she doesn't know how to protect herself and the boys don't know either. There are dangers now of very serious diseases that are sexually transmitted. I imagine you have classes at school about that."

"Actually we do, mom, but I never ask any questions because, you know, with boys in the class and everything it's embarrassing, so none of us pretty much ask any questions. We just listen. I do hear about AIDS, but gee, mom, none of the kids I know would have AIDS."

But her mother responds thoughtfully. "Well, then, you don't really know about AIDS. I have a little book here on it. Go over to the bookcase and there on the second shelf, third from the right you'll see a small book. Take it out, honey."

Her daughter jumps up and gets it.

And her mother continues, "Now I suggest that you read it. You will read about the ways a person can get AIDS, and you should know about that so as to protect yourself. But this girl is taking chances. And AIDS isn't the only thing. There's also herpes, darling, and other sexually transmitted diseases."

"Yes, yes we heard about that."

"In the same little book I've given you, there's a chapter on herpes, and the other diseases, and you have to learn about them too, so as to be knowledgeable, and so as not to risk your own well-being, ever."

"Oh, gee, mom, thanks a lot. After I read it, is it OK if I ask questions?"

"Most certainly. I hope you do."

"Then I'm going to read it tonight, mom."

"OK, honey."

Then her daughter looks at her and says, "Gee, mom, you really are super. You really do understand."

"Well, yes. Thank you for saying I'm super. And yes, I think I do understand, at least I try to understand. And this much I do know— that having sex before you really have learned how to choose your partner and have learned that you truly love your partner is not very successful. It's not really that enjoyable over the long run. And sometimes it spoils sex for a young person, because, like the young friend in your class, she is having sex when it is entirely physical and not connected with loving someone special very, very much. It has nothing to do with being really good best friends with that person, as well as loving him. So, remember, first learn to be good friends, trusting friends, friends who really like each other, and then maybe it's safe to begin to consider loving that person."

"Oh, mom, this I do know, just like you said, when you know you love someone, you don't have to ask, 'How do I know?' And I do love you." She throws her arms around her mother's neck and gives her a big kiss. Then she jumps up and says, "Well, I gotta go now, I'm meeting Pete at the library. So long."

And that's the end of the episode.

What If
Nobody Asks Me?

This is a story that begins in a room, a lovely room in a pretty house. Sitting in an armchair there is a handsome woman who must be the mother. And sitting with her is a charming adolescent girl who seems to be, oh, perhaps 16. The daughter is talking to her mother and looking a little worried, as she says, "You know, mom, it's only a month before the junior prom at school, and no one has asked me yet."

"Oh, are they asking this far ahead?"

"Well, Mary's been asked, but of course she's been going steady with Bill, and so has Ruth been asked, but then, yeah, she's been friends with Jack for some time now. And, you know me, I haven't really had a steady boyfriend, Mom."

Her mother smiles and responds, "No, I know that. But you've had your share of fun, and you've been asked to lots of things, and I don't see that you've missed many opportunities to go out. Isn't that right?"

Her daughter smiles a little, but still looks anxious. "But Mom, it would just be awful if I don't get asked to the prom!"

"Well, honey, I think a whole month ahead is a little too soon to be worried about it, don't you?"

"No, mom, that's all they talk about at school. All the girls are worried."

"Oh, you mean that most of the girls haven't been asked yet?"

"Yeah, that's right, but that doesn't help, mom. I know what you're saying, but all the same, what if nobody asks me?"

Her mother looks at her and smiles. "And that would be terrible, wouldn't it . . . the end of the world!"

"Oh, mom, you know what I mean! It wouldn't be the end of the world, but it wouldn't be much fun. It really wouldn't be much fun, and I am worried, mom."

Her mother reaches over, takes her hand, and holds it in both of hers, saying, "Honey, how about starting to worry a week from next Tuesday, and until then, just be your happy self? Very likely, right this minute, some young man in your class is sitting there talking to his dad, saying, 'Gee, dad, I'd like to ask her, but I don't know . . . she's so popular, and I don't know whether she would turn me down, and I would feel . . . ' And his father is saying, 'Well, if she's so popular, you'd better not wait. You'd better be in there first!' "

Her daughter laughs, and they are having fun with the idea when the phone rings. Mother answers it, saying, "Hello . . . oh, yes. . . . Well, how are you, Pete? . . . Yes, she's right here!"

Her daughter's eyes get big, and she mouths to her mother without making a sound, "He's gorgeous!" and then she hugs her mother tight before picking up the phone. She takes a deep breath and says, "Hello," then, "Oh, hi, Pete, how are you? . . . Oh, I'm fine, thanks . . . mmm . . . yeah . . . uhhuh . . . oh! . . . oh, I'd love to . . . that's wonderful . . . oh, thank you for asking me. I'd be delighted. OK! . . . All right . . . yes. Well, I'll see you at school tomorrow. Mmmhummm . . . no, I'm not in a hurry . . . no, it's OK." And so she settles herself down, curling up into a corner of the sofa.

Her mother looks over and mouths the word, "Prom?"

Her daughter nods her head vigorously, grinning from ear to ear. Her mother tiptoes out of the room.

And that is the end of the story.

Junior Prom

This is a story which takes place in a very pleasant, attractive household. The mother and father are sitting in the living room chatting together a little uneasily, obviously full of anticipation. The doorbell rings, and mother jumps a little, then laughs and stands up saying, "Well, I guess this is the big moment. Shall I let him in, or will you?"

Father replies, "Oh, let's go together." At the door, dad reaches out and opens it. There stands a very tall, very uneasy young man in a rented tuxedo, with a pre-tied bowtie. His hair is carefully combed, and his face is scrubbed rosy and shiny. He is really a very handsome young man. Dad says, "Hello, Pete. Come on in."

Pete holds out his hand, saying, "Good evening, sir . . . ma'am," and steps into the house.

Mother says, "Our daughter will be ready in a few minutes, I think. I'll go and see."

Her husband and Pete go into the living room and sit down. Mother disappears upstairs as the father starts a conversation. "Well, Pete, how is junior year going for you? Are you concentrating on anything in particular? Is there some special field of interest for you?"

"Uh, oh, yes sir, um, I want to go to college as a pre-med student, so I am taking as many math and science courses as I can now."

"Oh, I see. That's very interesting. So you've decided to be a doctor."

"Well, no sir, I'm not sure I want to be a doctor. You can do a lot of things with medicine besides being a practicing doctor."

Father is really interested now. "Like what? I mean, what do *you* want to do with it?"

[195]

"Well, sir, I thought maybe I could do research."

"My word! You are an ambitious young man!"

"I don't know about that, sir. I think sometimes I have a reputation for being pretty lazy. At least at home I do!"

Father chuckles. Just then mother comes into the room and announces, "She'll be down in a moment." She sits down to join them and almost immediately, rustling audibly, an apparition begins to descend the stairs. Three heads turn to watch her, and Pete stands up. Dad and mother stand up behind him. They all smile at the young woman coming down the stairs.

Indeed she looks lovely. She is in a beautiful dress that seems to float all around her. As she comes down, smiling and blushing, and looking quite self-conscious, she giggles and says, "Hi, Pete!"

Pete ducks his head and stammers, "Here, I brought you this." He holds out a white box.

Taking the box, she opens it, and produces a pretty corsage. "Oh," she says, "Wonderful! This is beautiful, Pete! Thank you so much! Where shall I pin it, mother?"

Mother asks, "Shall I help you?"

"Would you, please?"

Her mother pins the corsage on her shoulder strap.

The young woman goes over to the mirror and says, "It's just right, isn't it!"

Mother laughs. "Yes, it looks exactly right!"

Pete grins all over his face and then says, "Well, guess we ought to go now."

"Are you driving the car?" asks the young woman.

"Well, of course," Pete replies nonchalantly.

"Great! Let's go!"

Father says, "I know you will be very careful, right?"

"Right!" says Pete.

"And," Mother adds, "If there is some reason, later on, that you wouldn't want to be driving, you can call us, and we'll come get you."

Her daughter gives her a dirty look. Father grins, and the two young people look at each other in exasperation. Then they say, "Well, so long! We're off!" Daughter gives each parent a peck on the cheek, Pete shakes their hands, and with great relief they go out the door as the parents call out, "Have fun!" and they reply, "We will!"

This episode ends here, and now we skip to the end of the evening.

It is quite late. As a matter of fact, it is four in the morning. The young woman opens the front door softly, turns around and whispers

"Good night" for the fifth time. Pete sticks his face around the door and says, "Come on, come on, one more!"

She laughs. "Oh, you!" She leans forward to give him a brief kiss on the lips, and, as she turns away, to her embarrassment she faces her mother who has come down the stairs and is watching. She hastily closes the door, turns around and says, "Mom, what are you doing up? It's late."

"I *know* it's late! It's four in the morning! What are *you* doing up so late?"

"Oh, mom, some of the kids aren't going home at all. Most of them are going on to breakfast together. You know, on prom night you aren't supposed to go home."

"Oh, is that so? Well, I know we didn't set any curfew, but I certainly never dreamed it was going to be four in the morning."

"Oh, for heaven's sake, mom. Didn't you have a junior prom?"

"Well, yes. I did."

"And did you go home at midnight, like Cinderella?"

Her mother hesitates, then admits, "As a matter of fact, no."

"When *did* you get home, mother?"

"Well, actually, I stayed on, and we all had breakfast. So I take it back, my daughter. I was just worried, and I forgot about how it was when I went to the prom." Then she smiles and continues, "Well, did you have a good time?"

"It was wonderful!!!"

"Do you want to tell me a little about it now?"

"Oh, mother, I know you are going to laugh, but Pete is so . . . wonderful!"

"So that's how it is!"

"Oh, yes, mother, he is so, oh. I just can't express it! He is just terrific!"

Her mother bursts out laughing. "'Terrific,' is it?!"

"I think I'm in love, mother!"

"OK, OK, I hear," says her mother. "I'll tell you what. Let's go upstairs and I'll help you get out of these things, and I'll tuck you in. You have a good night's sleep, and then about noon we'll figure out whether or not you're really in love, OK?"

"Oh, mother, I'm really in love!"

"OK, darling, I understand. Up we go."

And that is the end of the episode.

Senior Prom

In this episode a young man dressed in a dinner jacket returns home. Coming up the front steps, looking very pleased and quite excited, he ushers in a charming young woman who is dressed in a pretty party dress. She's young and fresh and a little uneasy. But she is smiling and very eager to please.

They come forward and the young man says to his parents standing in the front hall, "Mom, dad, we stopped by so you can see how we look!"

And the young man's mother smiles at her and says, "You look lovely, my dear."

And his father says, "Pretty as a picture."

The young woman blushes, looks up at her escort who looks down at her, puts his arm around her waist, and says, "It's unanimous."

Awkwardly they stand there for a moment. Then dad says, "Well, I hope that you have a wonderful time at the prom. I know it's a big night for you."

And his son says, "Yep, it is . . . almost over. It's been quite a year."

And mom says, "Yes, an important year."

And then her son says, "Well, I guess we ought to get goin'."

So, in a flurry of excitement and laughter and good-byes and have-a-good-times, they leave the room. They go down the hall with mother and father following after, looking at each other, beaming. The young pair goes out the front door, turns once, waves gaily, and disappears.

Mom and dad turn away. Dad looks at mother and she looks at him. Spontaneously they embrace and they kiss gently. She says, "End of a chapter, beginning of another."

[198]

Dad says to her, "You know, I get all the signals lately that our son is quite smitten."

His wife looks at him, smiles and responds, "Oh yes, and she's really a very charming young woman. I think he's making a good choice."

Happily they go back to the sitting room together, and that is the end of the episode.

The next scene occurs about two o'clock in the morning. The front door opens, creaking a little, and the young woman comes in, turns around and holds her fingers up to her lips in a hushing gesture. The young man follows her in. He looks a little in disarray. His hair is mussed up and his collar is slightly crooked. She looks charming but also a little disheveled. They go in and sit on the sofa together. He puts his arm around the back of the sofa. She wiggles a little. He bends his head down toward her and she turns her face to him. His arm drops and he puts it around her and she holds her face up to be kissed. They kiss a long lover's kiss until finally she pushes him away. She's flushed and he's even redder.

She says, "Oh, we really should say good night. It's very late and I don't want my mother or my father to hear."

"They haven't heard anything. They're sleeping." He pulls her to him and there's a little struggle. Then she gives in for a moment and they kiss. His hand finds her breast.

She sits bolt upright, takes his hand away and says, "No."

But he pulls her close and says, "No?'

She says, "No!"

"Why not?"

And she replies, "Because."

And he asks, "What harm can it do?"

And she says, "I just don't want to do that now."

"Why not?"

And she repeats, "Because."

"Don't you want to be my girl?"

"Right now I'm not sure."

Then he says, "Oh, come on! Have you forgotten what you said the other day?"

"No."

"Well then . . . ?"

"Well . . . I just don't know."

"Well, OK, OK," he sulks.

She looks at him. "Don't be mad, Pete. I do like you a lot."

[199]

"LIKE!?" he says scornfully, "LIKE?"

"Well, maybe I'm even beginning to love you too, but I'm scared."

"Well, that's all right," he whispers, grabbing her and holding her tight and putting his hands on her body.

Again she breaks away. "I don't want to do that. I'm scared. And I'm not ready."

"Well, OK then," he sputters, "OK then. I hear you. That's enough. You don't have to say it anymore." He jumps up and strides to the door.

After a moment's hesitation she says, "Good night."

He turns back: "Just like that?"

And she says, "Well . . . " and goes up to him and puts her arms around his waist. He puts his arms around her shoulders. She gives him a hug and a kiss on the cheek, and then she breaks away and runs upstairs. He lets himself out, but he has a grin on his face.

And that's the end of the story.

Graduation

This story takes place in the living room of a charming house. We see a mother and father with their teenage daughter . . . a young woman who is dressed in a cap and gown. She is bubbling with excitement, and her parents are smiling at her and each other.

She asks them, "Shall I untie the ribbon and unroll it?"

"Yes, please do! Let's see what it says!"

So she unrolls the diploma and the three of them crowd together to read what it says. Then mother and father look at each other, beaming with pride, and their daughter throws her arms around both of them at once, exclaiming, "Oh, it's so GREAT to be finished with it, and I'm so excited about everything that I'm going to get to do now!"

Her mother suggests that they sit down together and talk. She turns to her daughter and says, "We took pictures of you, dear, and just as soon as they are developed we are going to choose one to have enlarged, and we'll put it here in the living room in a place of honor to remind us of this wonderful day of your graduation, and how proud of you we feel . . . how very proud of your accomplishments, and especially proud of the speech you made, how well thought out it was, and how poised you were, and how graciously you accepted your congratulations! And even though we had heard your speech several times as you were rehearsing, it was different today as you stood up there on the platform in front of the big crowded auditorium. You seemed so grown-up and so very much in charge of yourself."

Her father smiles and winks at her, and then smiles at his wife. They are very, very happy, indeed.

Then their daughter says, "I know I have all summer before I take off for college, but now that I have actually graduated, it seems so much nearer! It seems real for the first time!" And then she looks from one parent to the other with a faint shadow of doubt beginning to cloud her eyes, and she says, "Oh, I think I'm a little scared about it, too."

Her mother replies softly, "Of course you are, dear. It would be very strange, indeed, if you were to start off on this great new adventure without feeling some anxiety."

"That's right, mom, that's true." Then her voice changes, and she adds, "But I'm not altogether anxious. I'm also very, very excited about being on my own, going to a strange place, and making new friends, and I think the whole thing is probably going to be great!"

Her parents nod in agreement, and exchange proud glances.

Then their daughter says, "Well, I really do need to go and take this costume off, although I must admit I feel very comfortable in it, now that it's all over." Her parents laugh with her as she adds, "I think I'll run upstairs now, and change, because you know, Pete is coming by and we're going out to celebrate." Then she stops and hesitates a moment, looking at them with concern. "Is that all right with you? I mean, uh . . . uh . . . you hadn't planned anything, had you?"

Her father shakes his head, saying, "It really is all right with us, because we had a notion you would probably want to join your class-mates tonight, and your mother and I thought that perhaps on Sunday we would have a little gathering here to celebrate. How would that suit you?"

"Oh, daddy, you are super, and you too, mom. You do think of everything." And with that, she tosses a kiss in the air in their general direction and, laughing, runs happily up the stairs.

Her mother and father turn and gently put their arms around each other. He whispers, "What a wonderful young woman she is."

"Yes," his wife whispers in return.

And that is the end of the story.

Epilogue

Reactions to Reparenting Stories

When the taped stories end, I frequently allow the tape recorder to continue to record the dialogue between the client and me. These interchanges often serve as a bridge between reparenting trances and supplementary work. Some dialogues are taped at the beginning of the course of treatment, some approximately midway, and others near the completion of reparenting. The particular dialogues included here have been selected from a large collection because these represent a good cross-section of typical reactions to the trances.

AFTER THE "BIRTH" STORY

Client: I feel like crying.

L.W.: Go ahead.

Client: I cried during that first part.

L.W.: I know.

Client: I think I thought it was me, that I was the baby and I think that it felt sort of sad. I also felt that it was a happy story so I don't know where one started and one stopped. I don't think that I thought I was the mother until later. In the beginning I thought that I was the baby and then later I think I was the mother, but when I thought I was the baby that's when I cried.

L.W.: Why did you cry if you were the baby?

Client: I think that's what I didn't think my mother did for me and I felt sad. But it was also just kind of a nice story and I was sort of touched.

L.W.: Yes, mommy can be like that. You can be like that.

Client: That's an interesting thought.

L.W.: Not all mommies are like that. But, mommies can be like that. And you can choose that mommy. This is now.

Client: This is now. It really is now, isn't it?

L.W.: Yes. And you can choose.

Client: It's true. . . . Why is it that I feel I'm just waking up?

L.W.: Yes, you are waking up.

Client: Growth and change and the power of that is not . . . frightening isn't exactly the word for it. It's surprising. Not so fearful as it's just wonder, you know.

L.W.: Yes.

Client: You know, I start to think that maybe I will be not just a normal person but beyond that.

L.W.: Beyond a normal person?

Client: I mean, I always thought I was different from other people.

L.W.: In what way?

Client: I think I thought I was more sensitive, more intense, and I denied that. And now I think, I've always given normal people a bit of a bum rap.

L.W.: You didn't think you were normal? Did you believe there was something wrong with you?

Client: I was just different. It isn't all negative, just more stuff going on.

L.W.: And now?

Client: I think I denied that there was stuff going on for a long time in order to be like everybody else and now I think I can go ahead and have all the stuff going on, but just be more peaceful with it all.

L.W.: That you can accept how you are, is that what you're saying?

Client: Yeah. And that's nice . . . Do you understand what I was saying?

L.W.: Yes.

Client: I didn't know if I said it clearly.

L.W.: You said it very well.

Client: That's neat. This is nice, this is nicer than I thought it was going to be. I thought it was going to be awful.

* * * * *

[206]

AFTER THE "NEWBORN BONDING" STORY

Client: When I'm the mother it occurs to me, or maybe the baby, I'm not sure who, or me sitting in the chair, I'm not sure . . . I get the sense that I should be doing something else and then I go, "No, this is exactly what I'm supposed to be doing. I don't know who I am when I think that I should be doing something else." Then I think, "No, this is what I should be doing. This is what I need to do." Then I go back into being one or the other. Sometimes I'm one and sometimes I'm the other within the same story. And sometimes at the cuddling part in going to bed I just go back to being the baby. And I just let that happen and that's nice. That feels real good.

* * * * *

Client: I really visualize the story clearly. I see the story there. I see the movements of the baby. It's all very recognizable to me, and I've never had a child but I can see all this and the movements . . . yeah, amazingly real considering I've never really been around babies very often.

L.W.: You were once a baby.

Client: Right, right. I guess what you could say is that my conscious mind my immediate reaction is, you tell these stories to someone who has a separation disorder.

L.W.: What does that mean, "You tell these stories to someone who has a separation disorder"?

Client: There's a critical part of me that thinks, aren't you reinforcing? But, no, these are all the positive aspects of a mother, son, baby relationship. Rather than needing this stuff and looking for it later in life. It's very clear to me that this type of feeling is not something to be afraid of experiencing. That's right. That's what should happen when you're a baby. So it's very enjoyable. They're very pleasant. It's not quite the right word but they're very pleasant. The first time I thought about hearing a story about nursing, I went, "Ooooh, God, that's weird!" But they're very pleasant, happy stories. Does it make sense what I'm saying?

L.W.: Yes, wonderful sense.

Client: They seem very natural and very pleasant and very soothing and happy, and I keep thinking about how wonderful it is to

[207]

hear these stories in light of me considering being a parent. I think if you don't have any experience of good parenting, I think it's very hard to learn by yourself.

* * * * *

L.W.: Hi. How do you feel? . . . Take your time . . .

Client: I want to go back into the story.

L.W.: Take your time . . . you liked it there in trance. How was the weather outside when you first came in here today?

Client: You asked me that last time.

L.W.: It's not the same day. Take your time. You were really deep in there.

Client: It feels good. I want to go back to sleep.

L.W.: You weren't sleeping. If you were sleeping, how come you opened your eyes when I suggested you can open your eyes?

Client: I don't know.

L.W.: OK. Maybe you're still in another room.

Client: No, it wasn't the same room. I'm in a different room. I think I can make sense now.

L.W.: Well, you don't have to make sense.

Client: These are lovely stories. I get to be two things. I can be the baby and I can be the mother, and I go back and forth. I was the baby and that felt nice, and I was the mother and that felt nice. I like being both of them.

L.W.: I'm glad you're enjoying it.

Client: It's wonderful.

* * * * *

AFTER THE "BATH TIME" STORY

Client: My dad was kind of a nonparent for a long time. He ran away from the responsibility of the family into his work . . . ran away, literally, being on the road all the time through my high school years. He was gone two weeks at a time. His return was important to the family for a few moments, but almost at once he would bitch and moan about work, and there would be fights, and all sense of homecoming sort of flew out the window, because when he came home it was no better and no worse. It was just as bad. Of course, my mom being very sick, and with her alcohol problem, I was left to deal with her, to parent her, so I had to be a parent without even having a parent to model myself after. In terms of taking care of my mom, I would have to sort of just wing it. So, I found myself kind of relieved as I heard the stories. And it's funny, because once we started the infancy work, "B" commented on my changing, because at night instead of asking her, "Would you rub my feet, would you rub my neck?" I'd take care of myself; I'd rub my own feet; I would take care of my own self. I did it without noticing it. She pointed it out to me, and I went, "Oh, God, you're right. I AM taking care of myself a little better." That was the first time I realized that this work was affecting me in ways that I was unaware of.

* * * * * *

L.W.: Are you saying you are now more tolerant of your own perceived shortcomings?

Client: I think maybe I still fear my imperfections a little bit. They're hard for me to accept because I'm dealing with the question of just how good I am.

L.W.: How good do you have to be?

Client: Well, I don't know. The one thing I enjoy about creative enterprise, like composing or writing, is I always do the very best I can and it's always a surprise to me. So I guess that's as good as I have to be.

L.W.: That's a beautiful description of how good you have to be.

Client: I have to be open to what I can do. Otherwise, it doesn't make any sense. You can only be as good as you are. And to allow yourself that freedom is what I like about creative enterprise, because whenever I'm truly creative it takes me by surprise, and I'm always kind of amazed by it. Then I sit back and consciously look at what I've produced, and I go, "Well, how does it measure up?" I'm always going to have that part of myself. I call that the critic in me. I've got a critic. That's probably the last issue I need to deal with.

L.W.: What's the purpose of the critic?

Client: Well, a good critic should give you a point of view, should frame an artistic work and give it a point of view, I think, and put it in perspective to the world. I don't think a critic should ever be punitive, and when critics are punitive I really have a problem with it.

[209]

L.W.: And is that the standard you set for the critic in your own self?

Client: I try to. I've never really thought about it. It's very interesting. I've never thought about what role my personal critic should play in my life. I really do believe that a critic should offer a point of view, but I don't think they should injure an artist. I don't think an artist should ever be injured for really trying.

L.W.: And is that your standard for your own critic?

Client: Well it should be, now that I hear it.

* * * * *

AFTER THE
"BABY MAKES EYE CONTACT" STORY

L.W.: You feel sad?

Client: Yes.

L.W.: Do you have some idea what that's about?

Client: Yes. My father used to sing to me.

L.W.: And?

Client: I miss him.

L.W.: It's OK to cry. . . . That must have been a good experience for you, then, to hear daddy singing a lullaby.

Client: I liked being sung to. That's right. I just miss him, that's all.

L.W.: What is it you miss?

Client: I miss being sung to, and being loved like that.

L.W.: How can you be loved like that?

Client: It's not appropriate that I be loved like that now.

L.W.: It isn't?

Client: No.

L.W.: Sometimes we feel very little, and that's all right. It's all right to get comfort when we need it. It's all right to ask for it, to be held and to be rocked and to be sung to. Did you know that lovers do that?

Client: Not sung to, I don't know about that.

L.W.: Oh yes, lovers often sing. There are some beautiful songs that lovers sing. Do you know the song, "The first time ever I saw your face. . . . "

Client: Is that a lullaby?

[210]

L.W.: Sounds like a lullaby, doesn't it? "I thought the earth moved in my hand. . . . and I knew our joy would fill the earth and last till the end of time." Do you ever sing to "F"?

Client: No.

L.W.: Do you ever hold him, cradle him?

Client: I did last night but I didn't sing to him.

L.W.: Do you and "F" have some songs you both like?

Client: No.

L.W.: No songs?

Client: Oh, we have music that we like.

L.W.: Perhaps you can get some songs.

Client: That are "F" and my songs?

L.W.: Sure, you know, "They're playing our song." Have you heard that expression?

Client: Yeah.

L.W.: In trance, I sang your daddy's song that was "our song," so there can be a song that's yours and "F"'s. There can be several songs. It's lovely to sing in bed.

Client: We never did that.

L.W.: Do you ever play music when you're in bed?

Client: Yeah, sometimes.

L.W.: Well, you can get some with words you both like. You can get a song or two that are yours.

Client: Oh that's a nice idea. I like that.

L.W.: Did you think that you could never be cuddled and sung to anymore . . . ?

Client: I would do it to myself sometimes.

L.W.: OK. Sure. You can ask "F" to sing a song that you sing to yourself. What do you sing to yourself?

Client: The song my dad used to sing me when I was little. "Lullaby, now close your eyes, sandman's coming by. Dream sweet dreams, my baby, go to sleep in daddy's arms, sleep tight, sleep all night, go to sleep my baby, go to sleep in daddy's arms, sleep tight all through the night.'

L.W.: That's beautiful. Do you know the music to it?

Client: Yeah.

L.W.: Can you sing that to "F" sometimes when he needs it?

Client: Yeah. Yeah. That's right, I can do that, yeah. And there was another one, "Go to sleep, little darling, go to sleep. When you wake you'll have some cake and five or six little horses."

[211]

L.W.: Horses?

Client: Cake and horses, yeah.

L.W.: That's a lovely one. I like that.

Client: I think those are the only ones he sang.

L.W.: Well they're good ones. The one I always loved was the one, "Loo loo loo loo loo loo bye bye, up in mommy's arms be creeping, and soon you'll be asleepin', singing loo loo loo loo loo loo bye."

Client: Oh that's nice, yeah, you sang that once in the trance.

L.W.: "You want the moon to play with, and the stars to run away with, singing loo loo loo loo loo loo loo bye."

* * * * *

Client: I know I must be getting something from the stories because a couple of times after we've done work here, something new happens in my life, and of course I don't even remember what goes on here.

L.W.: Your unconscious knows what goes on here.

Client: That's interesting. That's happened twice: the eye contact with my mother, and my desire right now not to have contact with her, not feeling like that's what I want right now. And both related to work that we were doing. And what's so funny about it is I don't even remember what the story was about.

L.W.: Does that feel good?

Client: Yeah.

L.W.: Then you remember it in ways that are good for you.

Client: Now I'm already starting to forget.

* * * * *

AFTER THE "SEPARATION" STORY

Client: Well, the thing is that I no longer play mother to her. That's it. And I don't react as though her demands are reasonable and she has it coming to her that I give her all of this special consideration and attention. She has acted in the past as though she were my deprived child, you know, and that I was not being a good momma to her! That's really backwards. And I always accepted that I was supposed to be her parent, and had duties to perform. But that's over now I don't feel that way, I feel perfectly comfortable saying, "You'll be the first to know when I invite you, mom. Until then you'l have to wait."

* * * * *

Client: Once when I was in a school performance, singing a song, I looked down into the front row and my mother was there singing the song out loud with me exactly as I was singing it because she had memorized it, too.

L.W.: She was not differentiated from you.

Client: No. The other thing that occurred to me is that I think the biggest sabotage of success for me has been this dichotomy I have of either I will be protected only if I don't venture out, but if I venture out and do my own thing, then I'm going to give up the fatherly protection. There will never be anyone there for me, to love me. That I'm totally on my own, and "rocks of ruck, kid."

L.W.: There will never be any other "Daddy"?

Client: I have this vision of myself: I am much calmer than I used to be, not so frantic as I used to be, and I guess that comes from just accepting who I am and what I want.

L.W.: Yes. Becoming your own person.

* * * * *

Client: I went to this meeting on Saturday with these women, and people were really moved by what I had to say, and I don't think I've ever said anything that moved anybody before, and it made me feel like I'd made some progress.

L.W.: What really moved them?

Client: I've been keeping myself busy for so many years that I sort of cut myself off as a woman, as a person. I didn't put a lot of energy into being me. And then, I began to let myself feel. I just had never realized you've got choices. I just thought you did what a good girl did, and so you did it and it wasn't really an option for you. Then I talked about "that was then and this is now," that I don't have to be that way. I can choose to do something else. They were really moved by that.

* * * * *

[213]

AFTER THE "PLAYGROUND FIGHT" STORY

Client: During the end of the story, as you're closing up the story, and we were leaving, I had a very interesting thought. I thought, "Gee, I wonder if daddy and this lady will have an affair?"

L.W.: How did you feel when you thought that?

Client: Excited by the possibility. I think it has to do with . . . I can remember my dad saying, taking me down into the basement and saying, "You know, your mother and I might split up; you know, we might get divorced." I think he was trying to prepare me for the worst. And I really can remember thinking, being a little embarrassed by him telling me this. . . . I must have been all of six years old, and I'm thinking, "Good! Do it! Shit, or get off the pot. Do SOMETHING!" I didn't have those words in my mind but I remember having that feeling, "So good, do it." Because my mom was quite a mess at that point in our lives. She was heavily medicated and drinking a lot, and she kept falling down and injuring herself, you know. I can remember big gashes, big bloody gashes on her face, where she would fall in the bathroom and hit the sink. And you know, he was not there to care for me, or for her, and she needed a lot of care. She needed a lot of help and I was the only one there. And so I think that's what prompts my thought in the story. "Ooooh, a healthy woman!"

L.W.: He was going to provide you with a good mommy.

Client: Yeah, who takes care.

L.W.: In your trance life, you have a good mommy.

Client: Yeah, and that was very much me thinking as a looker at the story. The little boy didn't think that. It was me aware of my own life, commenting on that. Yeah, the good mommy is in my trance life. That's very . . . I'm very moved by all this. Very interesting, very interesting. The power of stories just blows my mind.

* * * * *

AFTER THE "WHEN I GROW UP, DADDY" STORY

Client: I feel good. That felt good. But this whole thing is all so very threatening.

L.W.: Threatening?

Client: My movement, not standing still, you know . . .

L.W.: What is threatening to you?

Client: Growing is threatening to me; changing is threatening to me.

L.W.: How are you growing?

Client: I don't know, doing things different.

L.W.: What are you doing differently?

Client: I don't know right now. I'm out of it; I can hardly talk about it.

L.W.: OK. Don't try to think.

Client: Since I feel I'm here, I think I m supposed to say something.

L.W.: You're not supposed to say something unless you want to say something.

Client: It feels good to just do this, though. I don't feel like doing anything else.

L.W.: That's exactly what you're supposed to do . . . what you feel like. But you did say that it's a little threatening to you, all this growing you're doing.

Client: I'm talking about the other stuff.

L.W.: What other stuff?

Client: Being honest all the time and all that stuff.

L.W.: Ohhh, yes. That's hard.

Client: It is hard. Being honest and not lying to myself.

L.W.: That's harder than anything, because we get a habit of doing that to protect ourselves. And when we do find out "that was then and this is now" and we don't have to fool ourselves, it's still a little scary to let go.

Client: That's hard. I watch that a lot. Now I'm aware when I'm not telling the truth. I feel real dishonest talking to my mother because I feel so angry, like I just don't want to play these games anymore. And I don't know what to do with that. Do I tell the truth?

L.W.: Yes.

Client: I thought about doing that. But when you start telling the truth, it's hard to have a relationship that you lie in all the time. And I lie in that relationship all the time. I feel angry that I have to lie.

L.W.: Who said you have to lie?

Client: It's either that I lie or I tell her how much I hate her.

L.W.: Is it either/or?

Client: I feel hate right now.

L.W.: Anger is different from hate.

[215]

Client: Is it?

L.W.: Sure.

Client: All right, I feel anger.

L.W.: You may feel angry because of what she does and because of what you do in response. But you don't hate her.

Client: I came close.

L.W.: You don't hate her or you wouldn't transact with her.

Client: Oh.

L.W.: You don't have to hate her to tell her the truth. By being honest, perhaps for the first time, you'll show that you respect her and yourself too much to lie.

Client: Oh. . . .

* * * * *

AFTER THE "GOLDILOCKS" STORY

Client: You know, I'm continually easier about dealing with my parents. My interaction with them, although it's important to me, seems less important. I like them and we get along, and it doesn't matter as much to me that everything be OK, and there aren't always problems to deal with, which is good. I'm getting better at accepting them as human beings. When I do that, I can accept myself better, too. I seem to accept that I also am not perfect, without beating myself up.

* * * * *

Client: I think I don't feel bad about my dad, completely, because when it came to things like . . . I don't know . . .

L.W.: When it came to things like what?

Client: Can't think of anything. He's a good social guy, a real fraternity guy, but I always saw through that, you know. He's the kind of a guy that says, "Hello, how you doing?" . . . and that's about as far as he goes . . . until you get to know him. He's a good conversationalist, though. He does know how to talk to people.

L.W.: I wonder if you remember now, that when you first came to see me, your dad was the one you were fond of and felt sorry for, because you thought he had been so abused and mistreated, and had lacked love from your mother. And that your mother

[216]

was the one who was at fault ... and now, it seems that it's neither one.

Client: Right, right.

* * * *

AFTER THE "MASTURBATION" STORY

Client: In school when I began to feel like I was going crazy ... I mean I knew I had some emotional problems related to my past, and I started knowing that I needed counseling, and knowing that I was facing some emotional crisis that evidenced itself in my relationships, my sexual relationships. What I wanted to know was how to be a man, I guess. How to be strong, how to be tough, how to express my feelings, my aggression. A lot of my life has been learning to express my aggression in a way that is useful and not destructive to myself, because when I was young, I tended to express my aggression in ways that were not useful to me. Didn't get what I wanted. That hurt me and embarrassed me, and a lot of my life has been spent learning how to ask for what I want in a way that will help me get it. I understand that now. It's amazing how I'm beginning to see the difference in how I get what I want.

L.W.: What is the difference?

Client: I'm not as scared to ask for what I deserve, I guess. I had a profound experience last Sunday. There was a matinee of this play that I'm in and I came to the theater and it always happens that when reviewers show up I often spot them before the show. If I don't see them, I'm fine. Well, I saw this reviewer from the "News," who has given me good reviews and bad reviews ... actually, just bad reviews, and it scared me because I've never met him and I figured he's a jerk. So, all through the first act I felt kind of under water. "Well," I said, "For Christ's sake go up and talk to this man, introduce yourself, say, 'Hello, thank you for the nice article on children's theater'", that he did last week. So I did, I chased him around during intermission, and I caught him, and I said, "You're so and so. Thank you for that nice article." We talked. Well, once I faced my fear, I just sailed through the second act. I was inspired and I realized it was facing what I was afraid of and that what I wanted was to know that he was a human being, and not this archetypal reviewer in this paper, "News." Big deal! It ain't going to ruin my career. So what I wanted was to feel comfortable. And what I needed to feel comfortable was to face something that was really very scary to me. To go up and introduce yourself to a reviewer during the intermission. That's pretty wild, but I did.

L.W.: And was he cordial?

Client: Very nice, just as scared as I was. He was just as nervous and happy to meet me as I was to meet him.

* * * * *

Client: As I was coming out of trance I saw . . . this is very weird . . . I saw this male face right in front of me while I was coming out of trance, this male face, and I kind of moved to the side, and I realized it was me, this face looking . . . I was asking, "Who is that guy? Oh, it's me!" It was a very pleasant image. It was a male face. It did kiss me in the fantasy, this male face. I feel somewhat shy about telling you that now. I felt like . . . well, at first, when I was trying to figure out the image, I thought to myself, "Well, oh, who's that guy kissing? Oh it's me! I thought it was a response to this work here, a sort of embracing of myself. An embracing of my father that becomes myself.

L.W.: Incorporating your parent?

Client: Yeah.

* * * * *

Client: The work we are doing with reparenting has been making a big difference. I'm reaching out more to make friends. I think I enjoy spending time socially. I used to feel very uncomfortable, like an outsider, worrying about whether people liked me. Now I even like to go out with friends. I seem to be calling them up more, not feeling so friendless.

* * * * *

AFTER THE "FATHER AND SON DISCUSS COURTSHIP" STORY

Client: I don't think I could have asked my fiancée to marry me without my new self-confidence. I don't think I depend on her so much. I'm more self-reliant. I can take care of myself better in the relationship. I used to equate love with taking care of another person, but now I only take care of her when she needs it, and it has more meaning for both of us. I used to think: "That's how you show you love somebody . . . you take care of them." And I don't think I do that anymore. What I want now is someone I can be honest with and who understands me, and whom I can talk to, and we can have a real dialogue. We can be aboveboard, and we can have some compassion. I really have that now with her. That seems to make all the difference in the world in our day-to-day life. And also sexually, you know. It takes all the pressure off. It is beginning to be an expression of love and not of performance, which s really the key for me.

* * * * *

Client: I have been very, very content with my accomplishments lately. You know, I have found great success in teaching, I really am a good teacher. And you know, you hit hills and valleys when you teach. You feel like your students don't know what the hell you're talking about. But now, finally, I have the impression that they're understanding what I've been talking about, which is reassuring. And that is surprisingly moving to me . . . it's inspiring to me, to see that change happen. And I was talking to "S" and I told her that up until now I've always thought that teaching would be a defeat in my life.
L.W.: Well, it's a parental role, you know.
Client: Oooooh, yes, you're right! (Chuckles) That's true.

* * * * *

Client: I've learned that creative projects have a life of their own, they really do . . . a point at which they take over and you're no longer directing everything. You can chip away, but still a piece of music has a life of its own that you need to respect, and you can give that lip service and understand that from a creative standpoint. But also you need to understand that from a personal standpoint, and in terms of humanity, that events and life and all human beings, you know, they have a life of their own. Things are going to happen and you can't control everything every minute of the day. You just can't do it. . . . You can only have so much impact on all of that. And once you realize that, then it takes the pressure off. What it does is it allows you to let a performance have a life of its own. You let other people do their work and you do yours. That's one thing that's hard to get across to kids. They're constantly directing each other. They don't talk in terms of themselves. They talk in terms of, well, "they should" or "you should." Do your own work, don't worry about others. You need to do your own work. And if you can get kids to do that, that's the first big step in becoming a "pro." Do your work; leave everyone else alone.

L.W.: Do you understand that what you're doing is parenting them in a very fine way?

Client: Oh, I have a real sense of that, working with the kids this time. I feel that I am a good parent. It's really gratifying. I had no idea it would be. I kind of poo-pooed that part of teaching. I had never experienced it happening so it didn't mean much, how you can really make a difference in someone's life.

L.W.: I'm wondering if you and "S" will someday decide to have your own children.

Client: Yes, I think we will.

* * * * *

Client: My attitude toward women underwent a change. I think that, when I started, my attitude toward women was mistrustful and seemed to be full of conflict. I think I have continually made poor choices in whom I was attracted to and whom I went out with. I think I picked angry little girls who took out their anger on me. "T" is so different from anybody I've ever gone out with. I mean, I always felt very sexually threatened, like I had to perform or I was a failure, and it gave me a lot of anxiety sexually. I don't feel any of that with "T." I feel like what we have in our relationship is always right there to be seen—no hidden agenda. If there's a problem we talk about it, and we're honest, and honesty is a big, *big* difference in my life.

I was never really honest with myself and I was never really honest with anybody. I was scared to be honest. For example, I used to, if I didn't feel like going out with some friends and I

[220]

had an appointment to go out with friends or a date to go out with friends, I would call and say, "Oh, my car just fell apart," or, "I'm sick," or, "Something catastrophic has happened," so I wouldn't do it, so I wouldn't have to go out. Now, if I don't want to go out, I call people up and I say, "Listen, I'm just too tired. I don't want to go out tonight. So can we reschedule?" And lo and behold, the sky doesn't fall, so that's an example of being honest.

I'm more honest with myself about money, about how much I really have, about how much I really need. "T" and I used to have financial problems, I always used to borrow cash from her and then have trouble paying it back. Now we're pretty much stable I mean, she borrows ten bucks every now and then and I borrow ten bucks every now and then, but we pay it right back and keep square and that's a difference. At first, there were problems I think with our being able to communicate, problems that surfaced to the point that we knew if we wanted to stay together we needed to deal with them.

But see, there's the big difference. And see, I had never experienced that in my life. All the problems that came up in my family life were never dealt with. You just went on with the problem manifesting itself in behavior and never resolving. And I always picked women who were not willing to resolve the problems of communication or whatever that came up in the relationship. So rather than continue the relationship it would end up fizzling out painfully. It's not that I have a problem with opening my heart to somebody That's never been difficult for me, but I always picked women who weren't able to work through the mechanical problems and communication problems of a relationship that would then enable an easy flow of feeling. Well, "T" was able to do that and that's the huge difference. Mature, honest, reasonable, all those adjectives describe our relationship. See, the thing about the reparenting that's very interesting to me is that "T" keeps saying to me, "God, you've changed so much." I know that I've changed, but I kind of see it as a whole thing as opposed to this and this and this are different. It's just a general ease of life. So it could be the reparenting . . . learning to take care of yourself.

* * * * *

[221]

Client: Three colleges asked me to teach in September. They liked the rapport I had with the students so much. And I think the continuing work is due to the success I've had with classes. I've taught four classes and they all were very successful. That was a new thing for me, scary but exciting. And I think that one of the things that reparenting has done for me as a teacher is that I'm as good a parent as a teacher. I just found myself able to take charge. I used trancing a lot before teaching. I would trance and that seemed to clear my mind and help me to be spontaneous. A lot of what I teach is improvisational. You have to kind of go with the flow of the class and pick exercises spontaneously that are going to motivate and make the points.

And through the course of teaching four different courses, I've developed, now, one course that I'm going to teach. My standard basic course is now complete with teaching materials, and a workbook, and all that has been developed. But that took teaching and experimenting with four different classes. Now I've got a standard basic course I can teach which is kind of a neat way to do it.

And one thing that teaching enforces in your life is a sense of order. There are schedules made far in advance and . . . I used to feel rebellious about schedules, but now I see the necessity of it, and it's not that difficult. It makes it kind of easy. Your life is a little more ordered. The class was kind of developed in my old way . . . crisis after crisis. I'd rush in, teach and, oh well, I'd come up with something. But now it's all in files and it all makes pretty much sense. Yeah, it's much easier to have an organized program.

* * * * *

AFTER "FIRST SEXUAL ENCOUNTER" STORY

Client: My parents were not particularly enabling. I was not given a way to feel good about being independent and venturing away from parental protection, and also in high school years, not given a way to make my best decisions. I mean, I suppose that I imagine that there is a way to parent a child so that they are given options, and they really feel like they make their own decisions, but they're guided in such a way as to give a child the ability to choose for themselves and to feel good about that choice and to empower that decision. To choose the best, because who knows what's best for somebody except yourself? The ability to choose and feel good about making the choice, and following through and all that kind of stuff. And I realize that I'm in a pretty good place at age 26. My parents must have done something right, because here I am, able to at least decide for myself at this age.

* * * * *

Client: Now I feel like I'm doing a pretty good job, at age 32. Here I am . . . able to at least focus my life. I have enough sense of myself to guide myself my own way now, and so I end up trying to forgive my parents.

L.W.: Have you forgiven them?

Client: I think so. Here I am . . . making all these changes. I just think I have to accept the fact that they did the best they knew how. I seem to feel easier about things . . . softened . . . I don't feel so angry.

* * * * *

Client: I think I'm feeling much calmer than I used to be, not so frantic. I guess that comes from just coming out of who I am and what I want. I was very angry with my father for not being there for me, and with my mother for not letting me do my own thing, for trying to do my living for me, not letting me be me. It's like now, I don't consciously feel that angry. Well . . . now here I am, in my late twenties and doing pretty well. I'm here. So they must have done some good things. I just think you have to realize that they did their best.

* * * * *

AFTER "GRADUATION" STORY

Client: I remember when, while I was well into this process of reparenting with you, I went last summer and spent that one day with them [father and stepmother]. We went out for a drive and he was starting to give my stepmother a hard time or to tease her in some way that I thought was . . . he was pretending that it was in fun but to me it was very clearly unpleasant criticism. And I teased him real playfully, real playfully, with lots of delight on my face, and got him to laugh and drop it. And that was really fun. It was like I was not afraid of him. We were into this work, yeah, I had already done lots of peek-a-boo playing, lots of peek-a-boo with my imaginary father. I kept imagining that. It kept coming to me, that joy we had shared in session here . . .

L.W.: And you were able to show that to him.

Client: Yeah, so I didn't bring any defensiveness to that day.

L.W.: That's pretty nice.

Client: Very nice. Exactly the way it should be.

L.W.: So perhaps you have gained back a father . . . in a good way.

Client: Yeah, that and the graduation too.

L.W.: How do you mean?

Client: Well, the session we did where I graduated and was going off to school. I mean I remember that and carried that feeling of approval . . . the just wonderful sense of being loved and appreciated by my parents. That's just really with me, I love it. So I have a lot more space to bring to him, more psychic space of my own. I think that in the past I've probably been needy—needy of some of the things that he didn't have to offer. And so I reacted by being a demanding, unsatisfied self. And now I don't need anybody to offer me those things. They are incorporated, you know, that self-approval and self-love and sense of appreciation incorporated in me, you know, and so I bring a sort of spacious, gracious, relaxed, whatever is OK, don't-need-anything kind of energy. So, even if he is isolating himself, or can't sleep, and needs people to be quiet, or is grouchy, it doesn't affect me, because I'm not needing anything else from him. Big difference.

L.W.: That's beautiful.

Client: It really is, it really is.

* * * * *

In conclusion, it is my belief that reparenting stories have the power to heal basically because they enable clients to accept themselves as adequate and lovable. There is a recurring theme of forgiveness in the dialogues: "It wasn't that they didn't love me. They did the best they knew how . . . " And then there is the consequential forgiveness of self: "My best is good enough." The diminishment of anger, fear, and sadness makes room for trust, spontaneity, and love. Every child's birthright! Truly, it is never too late to have a happy childhood!

[224]